Lessons from Lucy

Elizabeth Huxtable

Manor House

Cataloguing in Publication

Title: Lessons from Lucy / Elizabeth Huxtable
Names: Huxtable, Elizabeth, author.
ISBN 978-1-988058-99-3 (hardcover) |
ISBN 978-1-988058-98-6 (softcover)
BISAC Subjects: BIO033000: Biography / People with disabilities. | BIO033000: Biography / Personal Memoirs

Art: Front Cover: Lucy / Back: Author Elizabeth Huxtable

First Edition
Cover Design-layout / Interior- layout: Michael Davie
190 pages / approx. 56,000 words.   All rights reserved.
Published 2023   / Copyright 2022
Manor House Publishing Inc. 452 Cottingham Crescent, Ancaster, ON, Canada L9G 3V6   (905) 648-4797)
www.manor-house-publishing.com

Description: An inspiring story of hope, strength and courage. After doctors said there was no hope for her newborn daughter, this mother refused to give up. Despite her daughter's severe disabilities, Lucy went on to touch many lives with her presence and became her mother's greatest teacher. Follow Elizabeth Huxtable's journey to create the best life for her daughter. In so doing, she discovers in herself latent talents, fortitude, resilience and ultimately, the greatest gift of all, the true meaning of unconditional love. Armed with these new skills, Elizabeth Huxtable has forged an international career as a sound therapist and healer.

*For all parents
struggling to care for
their special children*

Praise for *Lessons from Lucy*

"*Lessons from Lucy* is a very special true story about an expectant mother readjusting to the shock of giving birth to a "special needs" child, Lucy, who is completely dependent on her. Elizabeth Huxtable breathes life into the agony of expectations dashed and how she transforms them into her own powerful spiritual journey. In her exploration to find ways to help her child she transforms herself... an emotionally painful yet uplifting story." - **Virginia Kennedy,** Filmmaker.

"What this little girl was and is in spirit is absolutely amazing and needs to be shared with the world. That Lucy was non-verbal and still had such an impact on others is important. Elizabeth's story demonstrates how the unconscious can become conscious through what she experienced while parenting Lucy." - **Aaron Schultz**, author, *A Wink from a Guru*; Founder of The Outback Mind Foundation.

"This is a story of trust, wanderings, struggles, belief in one's self, belief in others, a story of challenges and triumph. A butterfly came into Elizabeth's life, showed her wings and flew away. This is the revelation of Spirit, where the human form is eclipsed by unlimitedness." - **Jain 108**

"... an extraordinary story of love, healing and transformation told with disarming honesty, crystalline lucidity and astonishing calmness. Elizabeth Huxtable writes from the heart, with guileless simplicity and sincerity, and before you know it, she has shown you how to transmute your own traumas into profound insight and heart wisdom. Like a trusted friend she gently guides you on an unexpected pilgrimage to an intimate and sacred space - your own innermost being... *Lessons from Lucy* is a book you'll want to share with friends and family. It will inspire and motivate you to heal your own emotional wounds..." - **Antares Maitreya**, formerly known as Kit Leee, is the author of four books and a number of blogs.

FOREWORD

I was honoured to be asked by Elizabeth to write a Foreword for this book. I am a published Author & have a history of working in the musical field as an Internationally published Singer/Songwriter, as well as an International Energy Healer & Spiritual Teacher in Holistic Alternative Therapies.

Amazingly I have lived in Daylesford, travelled in Egypt, have relatives that saw "Nessie" (Loch Ness Monster), love Mt Shasta & work with Mt Shasta energies, I am interested in film, have a narcissistic ex-husband who taught me much & the list goes on of Elizabeth & my life parallels. So parts of Elizabeth's story were like reading about my own challenges & life journey and once immersed in this journey, found I could not put it down.

This factual story is the definition of strength, devotion, courage & resilience. This is the story of a Mother who was able to transcend the Earthly trials of being the sole carer of a severely disabled daughter while appreciating the metaphysical & greater reasons, for the extraordinary gift that her daughter's existence, gave to her life.

It is a testimony to the power of the Human Spirit to rise to the occasion when life appears to be handing you seemingly insurmountable challenges and gaining the true rewards from these life lessons that have, in truth, been chosen by ourselves at a Higher level.

Lucy, the daughter's gracious Spirit shines through the physical encumbrances of a disabled body so we can perceive her grace, healing energy, spiritual awareness & love. Her incarnation, in fact, was an expression of unconditional loving 'presence' which we can all learn from and which often summoned the best in others.

While Elizabeth, the mother, navigates this hugely challenging life experience with insights, depth & wisdom that can only be gained & fortified through navigating a profound life journey such as this. Also teaching us how tapping into our own creativity can become a powerful resource in life and her evolution into a powerful Sound Therapist. Thus, Elizabeth illustrates a full life, well lived...

This book is such a valuable sharing because it teaches us to not only be grateful for what we have but how to view these experiences with a wider lens that can see the bigger picture.

This is a book that provokes deep inner reflection for what life journey we ourselves have chosen & how the Human Spirit when at it's best, is indefatigable indeed!
- **Medyhne Lebachen,** based in Australia, is a Mum, and Spiritual Teacher, practicing multiple healing modalities and energy healing (USA qualified Minister of Healing, a Reiki Master) with a global Clientele. She's a published Author; singer/songwriter; artist; international Radio Host (Healthy Life Network with a global audience of 3.5 million); ambassador of Oceania Restoration Council; founder of You Tube Channel "Arise Humanity" and founder of Soul Healing Group for Australia and is a spiritual entrepreneur. www.medyhne.com.

INTRODUCTION

Join Elizabeth on her Journey of vast experiences, visiting sacred sites, her many connections and some rejections, a marriage that went askew, delving into Seth material, moving interstate to access better services, trial and testing of traditional and alternative therapies, a bit of belly-dancing, her many moments of bliss, and some incidents that just don't go as planned.

The list goes on: telepathic communications between mother and child, the transmutation of grief that leads to the Higher Heart and Learning... Such was the case with the birth of her Lucy, her Light, her Teacher.

Share some of the most poignant moments when:

"her little hand closed around my finger."

Elizabeth's stories are profound. Consider this paragraph:

It was challenging for me to get any type of break from caring for her 24 hours a day. Thank goodness for an organization called, "Very Special Kids" (VSK). It was set up as a charity to give parents of children with life-threatening illnesses a break from the demanding role of caregiver. Staffed around the clock by nurses and an on-call doctor, it allowed parents a chance to relax and enjoy a few days' break without worrying about our children. On my first break, when Lucy was three years old, I went to the cinema for the first time since she had been born. It was such a delight to immerse myself in the story and completely forget about my caring role for a couple of hours."

Feel Elizabeth's soul as she describes the loss of Lucy and the mystery that lay ahead:

"I... was deeply grieved at losing the most precious person in my life. No more morning smiles, no more cuddles. I was heartbroken to have lost her. She had been my world for 10 years. Almost every waking minute she had been in my thoughts."

Elizabeth's life with Lucy, amidst all of its challenges and epiphanies, eventually leads her to discover her true calling:

It was via Lucy's need for multiple therapies that Music Therapy was introduced into Elizabeth's life, which put Elizabeth on a extraordinary path of Sonic Healing, and later, after Lucy's passing, catapulted her immersion into the invisible world of frequencies that heal.

Be touched by some of the moving and chilling stories in Elizabeth's life post Lucy's passing, the time she walks the Labyrinth at the Chartres Cathedral and Lucy in Spirit accompanies her!

Elizabeth, through her deep care for Lucy, achieved a form of Initiation, and her reward was finding her magic healing wand, her voice and the power of sound led her to the world of vibrational medicine, elevating her many karmic events to the exalted plane of spiritual service and mastery.

- Jain 108, author of more than 30 books on Sacred Geometry and Vedic Mathematics

Table of Contents

About the Author

Originally a research scientist and then an educator in Australia, Elizabeth Huxtable began her journey into complementary therapies 30 years ago. She is a qualified masseuse and Reiki practitioner.

More recently, after the passing of her daughter, Lucy, as she strove to heal from her own traumas, Elizabeth trained in a variety of modalities including energy psychology techniques, sound therapy and biofield tuning.

Due to her experience parenting a child with severe disabilities, Elizabeth has a keen interest in researching how sound therapy can benefit special needs children. She believes there is a strong link between emotions, mind and body and integrates all three aspects into her work. Children with special needs are often highly sensitive and are affected by the emotional states of those around them. Therefore, when working with the children, she also focuses attention on the parents.

Elizabeth is currently based in Kuala Lumpur, Malaysia, where she practices as a sound therapist, but also spends time teaching and working in Australia, South East Asia and Europe.

Chapter 1

Unconditional Love

The phone rings at 6:00 a.m. and I climb through layers of sleep and stagger out of bed to grab the cordless handset from the living room. No one calls at 6:00 a.m. unless it's an emergency. *Has Lucy been rushed to hospital after suffering another seizure?*

Yesterday had been my weekly day off from parenting and I had fallen gratefully into bed the previous night, eager to restore my energy for what lay ahead.

Lucy attended the Ballarat Specialist School for disabled children and at the end of her day a wheelchair bus had transported her to the respite home near the school where staff had been trained to care for her intense needs.

They would feed her special formula, mixed with her epilepsy medication, through a gastrostomy tube directly into her stomach. Then they would bathe her, put her to bed and send her to school the following morning.

I answer the phone and I'm surprised to hear the voice of the respite home manager rather than one of the staff members. "I'm so sorry to inform you that Lucy passed away overnight," she says. The words feel like a punch to the head. A scream involuntarily erupts from my throat and, suddenly, the phone line goes dead. The cordless phone battery is flat.

I continue to scream and wail. I lie on the floor curled up into a ball and cry the hardest I'd ever cried in my whole life. Only 36 hours earlier, I had ended my marriage to an abusive husband and now my only child was gone. As the crying subsides, numbness sets in. I don't know what to do with myself.

A few minutes later the doorbell rings. It's the local ambulance paramedic. His daughter is in the class Lucy attends at the local school two days a week. He is a kind and friendly man. He explains that the manager of the respite home thought I must have fainted from shock when she couldn't hear me anymore, so she phoned for an ambulance. I explain that the cordless phone simply ran out of battery.

This man is a Godsend; we sit down to a hot cup of tea, and I pour out my shock and confusion. I tell him about my healing session the day before. My friend had recently been trained in a technique to cancel the energetic, karmic, and emotional contracts we have with others, the ones that no longer serve us.

I had booked the session to clear any contracts I might still have had with my estranged husband. He had left twice before and then he had inveigled his way back into my life. I wanted to make sure I was energetically clear of him so that wouldn't happen again.

However, during the session, the contracts that came up for cancelling related to my daughter, Lucy. I didn't understand why I would be cancelling contracts with my 10-year-old daughter. She was totally dependent on me in every way. Now everything suddenly made more sense.

Over the previous few weeks, a peace I had never experienced had come over me each time I bathed her before bed. Previously, I had viewed bath time as a huge chore. I would start by undressing her on the hospital bed in which she normally slept. Lucy weighed 35 kilograms (about 77 pounds) and she was tall for her age;

I had found the only way to bathe her was to place a sling around her, lift her with an electric hoist attached to a ceiling beam, slide her along the beam into the adjoining bathroom, lower her into a reclining bath chair, and then kneel and strain my lower back washing her.

But lately, it had been different. The bedroom and bathroom had become like a holy sanctuary. Safe from my husband's anxiety and angry outbursts, this time alone with Lucy had become like a healing balm. I no longer saw the broken child that needed fixing. Instead, I felt her magnificence. She exuded powerful feelings of peace and calm.

A Sacred Silence

Our usual routine had seen me chatting and joking with her, then answering on her behalf in a sassy smart Alec-y voice, "Oh mum, don't be so ridiculous!"

But, lately, a kind of sacred silence had ruled over our nightly ritual. We had begun communicating telepathically. I didn't need to utter a sound. And I finally understood what unconditional love was.

I remember shedding tears of joy and awe as I telepathically told her how honored I felt to have the opportunity to serve such an incredible Being of Light.

Why had it taken me so long to reach this point? I wondered if it was possibly because my relationship with my husband had deteriorated so much: when it was just Lucy and I alone together the contrast was so extreme that

13

I felt myself transported into a higher dimension in her presence.

Her stepfather had come to resent those bath times. I never shared my revelations with him, but he could see me emerge from the room filled with calm and radiating peace.

He kept pestering me to ask the council to send home help more often than just once a week to do the bathing. But I did not want to give up those sacred nightly times.

As I talk with the patient ambulance driver over a third cup of tea, realization dawns on me: Lucy came to teach me what unconditional love is and I had finally learned it, finally fully embodied it, so her mission was complete, our contracts had been dissolved, and it was time for her to move on.

In my mind's eye I can see her dancing, free of her crippled body, dancing for joy over the fact that Mum finally "got it." And I sense very strongly that she waited until I finally rid myself of my narcissistic husband, once and for all.

Before this split, each time he had left I had felt unable to cope on my own so when he would apologetically come back, I had allowed him back in.

But this most recent time, I knew I would never take him back. I felt strong enough now to be Lucy's sole parent. And I felt his involvement represented a liability that far outweighed any practical help he may have given.

I could sense that my resolve to never take him back was the green light Lucy needed to go on her way, she knew that Mum was finally safe.

I recalled meeting a clairvoyant nine years earlier. She told me that in a past life, Lucy had been my guru. I had sat at his feet and said, "Now I understand what unconditional love is," and the guru had replied, "No, you don't understand it." The clairvoyant told me that my guru had come back in this lifetime to teach me what it truly was.

So, what have I learned? That unconditional love is about totally accepting what *is*, and not trying to change it. It's loving completely what *is*, instead of what I wish, or what I think *could* have been.

Thank you, my dearest Angel. You didn't only teach me this, you taught me so many other things as well.

Your life was a miracle, from start to finish. My life has been transformed by your presence as you helped me push through so many self-imposed limitations, empowering me in the process.

To those who looked only on the surface with pity in their eyes, you were a helpless, totally dependent child, unable to contribute in any way.

However, you helped me to question what it is to live a meaningful life and to make a useful contribution. I recognize that rather than being a curse, your presence in my life was the greatest gift a parent could ever receive.

Two of your old classmates, now young women, managed to track me down more than 10 years after you left us, to share how you had contacted them, one through a medium, the other through a meditation. Both received uplifting messages that touched their hearts.

Your legacy lives on.

Chapter 2

Getting Ready for Lucy

Prior to becoming a mother, I had lived almost as a nomad for two years, travelling the world with whatever I could fit into my backpack.

This nomadic lifestyle had been the antidote to an earlier life when, after 10 years working as a researcher in a chemistry lab, I had re-trained as a math and science teacher. Teaching at a government school in Darwin, northern Australia, however, had been a bad career move! I hated every minute of life in the system, forcing unwilling minds to learn algebra and trigonometry, and my stomach churned each morning on my drive to work.

I resigned from teaching with the idea that I would travel throughout South America for a few months, and include a trek along the Inca Trail to Machu Picchu in Peru as part of my itinerary. After reading several of David Hatcher Childress's books—including *Lost Cities and Ancient Mysteries of South America,* and *Lost Cities and Ancient Mysteries of Lemuria and the Pacific*—I was inspired to visit some of these ancient sites and experience the energies there. I felt a deep connection to the Andes Mountains—and with mountains in general.

I had trekked in the Himalayas several years earlier and had had an almost transcendental experience at one point in my journey. The energies at the Inca ruins in Cuzco and the Sacred Valley, and at Machu Picchu, had had a powerful effect on me and the people of Peru, Chile, and Argentina had been so warm and welcoming!

Spanish had been quick and easy for me to learn, especially since almost no one spoke English; learning the language had been a matter of necessity.

After my trip around South America, I returned to Australia - but it didn't feel like home anymore. I yearned to travel the world and explore sacred sites and energy portals. If I sold the property I owned, I reasoned, I'd be able to travel for a long time. Once I'd made that decision, the property sold effortlessly, and at the price I wanted.

With no fixed itinerary, I flew to England to visit the sacred sites of Stonehenge, Avebury, and Tintagel (thought to have been where King Arthur had his castle), and then on to Scotland, the birthplace of my maternal grandfather. There I explored Loch Ness and, in the very far north, the Orkney Islands with their mysterious stone circles.

I connected with a friend I had known in Australia who was also travelling throughout the UK. She really wanted to visit Egypt but was too nervous to go there alone. At first, I didn't want to join her, but she insisted, so we went for a couple of weeks. We spent a few brief days in Cairo and visited the pyramids at Giza. After spending time in the King's Chamber, I went into an altered state of consciousness and emerged from the pyramid feeling so spacy I could hardly function!

Next, we took an overnight train to Luxor. Luxor Temple with its feminine energy was connected to its twin temple, the more masculine Karnak Temple, by an avenue 2.5 kilometers long (about 1.5 miles) that was lined with ancient Sphinxes. I had a magical time. My friend was very sensitive to energies also, so we explored the temples, locating powerful energy spots. Luxor Temple particularly attracted me.

Four Marriage Proposals

My friend returned to the UK vowing never to return to Egypt, repulsed by the unwanted attention of the young Egyptian men. I, on the other hand, found it amusing to receive four marriage proposals in one day! And as I left I knew there was more for me to explore there.

I had booked a tour in East Africa that saw me visiting several game parks in Kenya, Tanzania, and Uganda, as well as the mountain gorillas in Zaire. And I decided to stop off in Egypt on my way back to London. This was a pivotal decision.

Back in Luxor once more, I met some tourists who were travelling upstream to Aswan on a traditional sailing boat known as a felucca. I decided to join them.

Sailing the mighty Nile River on a sailboat was delightful. Over the three days of the journey, we stopped off at several temples along the way, but nothing matched the energy of the temples in Luxor.

From Aswan we piled into old taxis at 3:00 a.m. for the long journey through the desert to Abu Simbel in order to arrive at sunrise. Abu Simbel Temple is famous for having been rescued before the Aswan Dam was finished. Rather than ending up underwater, the stones were meticulously moved to higher ground and the temple was rebuilt. I found it interesting that although the temple looked the same as its creators intended, I could not feel any energy there.

During the early morning drive, I lapsed into a state between waking and sleeping. Suddenly I heard a voice. It wasn't like a voice inside my head; it sounded like a man was beside me, speaking in my ear in a commanding voice, *"Write a book in the Luxor Temple!"*

This was not a suggestion; it was a command. I snapped out of my reverie. What had just happened? Excitement flowed through me. I'd always fancied the idea of writing a book but what was this book supposed to be about?

I was a fan of Richard Bach, author of *Jonathan Livingston Seagull* and *Illusions*, allegorical tales sharing spiritual insights via entertaining and often amusing stories. Maybe that was the kind of book I should write? Maybe I was going to channel a story? When discussing the writing of *Illusions*, Bach described how he had felt compelled to write, and the story simply flowed onto the page.

Another author I admired, Isabel Allende, had once been confronted by one of her readers who asked her why one of her characters suddenly murdered someone and she replied that she was shocked by the murder, too. She noted that after connecting with her Muse, her stories simply wrote themselves. She never knew what was going to happen; her characters took over. I was intrigued by this type of writing.

I shared my plan to write a book in the Luxor Temple and the locals warned me against doing it during the summer months, as summer in Luxor was unbearably hot. It was early spring, and they suggested returning in five months in the fall, sage advice as it turned out. What should I do for the next five months? Latin America was calling me, so I headed first to Mexico and then Guatemala to visit the Mayan sacred sites; then I travelled on to Peru where I walked the Inca Trail a second time. Next, I travelled to Chile where I visited some friends in the capital city of Santiago whom I had met on my previous trip a year earlier.

Returning to Luxor for the third time in October 1993 I found an apartment to rent and purchased a bicycle to make commuting between the apartment and the temple easier. I made an appointment to visit the Chief of Antiquities, explaining my plan to write a book in the temple. I asked if it was possible to get some kind of "season's pass" so I wouldn't need to purchase tickets every day and he generously offered me a free pass for one month; he patiently renewed it for 30 more days each time I returned to tell him that I hadn't finished the book yet. This happened eight separate times!

I wrote each day in the temple until the following May and the full force of the summer sun compelled me to leave. Once the temperature exceeds 50°C (122° Fahrenheit), government departments are obliged to allow their staff to leave work so, officially, it never gets hotter than 45°Celsius (113° Fahrenheit).

However, locals with thermometers reported that the temperature frequently exceeded 50°C. One day as I queued at the post office, I started to faint. It was 53°C (127° Fahrenheit). Fortunately, I knew the shop owner next to the post office who quickly revived me with a cool drink. He told me that the dizziness was caused by dehydration. I was drinking almost four liters (about one gallon) of water plus a large glass of sugarcane juice—which was full of electrolytes—every day. On that day, I had forgotten to drink a glass of water just before leaving for the post office. That had been enough to dehydrate me!

What Was This Book About?

The temple opened each morning at 6:00 a.m. and I was always the first to arrive on my bicycle with a cushion to sit on and a notebook. At first, I had no idea what I should write. What was this book supposed to be about? Did the mysterious voice that had commanded me to come intend to channel a book through me? I felt quite clueless. But in eight months, I filled eight notebooks, each with 100 pages. My chosen writing place was near the back of the temple where I would sit at the base of one of the columns.

When my friend and I had first visited the temple the year before, we had felt very strong energies in this part of the temple. However, several temple guards suggested I move to a small room adjoining this large breezy area. Sometimes a stubbornness in me surfaces. "Don't tell me where to sit, I'll sit where I choose," I muttered under my breath.

But something weird started happening. Out of the corner of my eye while I was writing I could see a tall being standing at the entrance to the small room, summoning me inside with a hand gesture. Each time I looked up directly there was no one there.

After this happened a few times, curiosity outweighed my stubbornness, and I entered the room. There were only four columns in this small room. The back wall was mostly gone so I could see the traffic in the street beyond the outer perimeter of the temple complex. Immediately, I felt a powerful energy in the room, so I sat and meditated and effortlessly slipped into an altered state of consciousness. I have never been very good at meditation, always struggling to quiet my mind, but in that room, I easily entered into the deepest meditative states of my life.

The added advantage of being in the small room was many tour groups never bothered to enter it. From time to time, a tour guide would bring in a group and describe hieroglyphs and friezes carved into what remained of the walls. However, mostly I had the room to myself. My routine was clear: 6:00 a.m. start with meditation and writing until 8:30 or 9:00 a.m. when hunger overcame me and I'd pedal home for breakfast. By that time, the temple was filled with busloads of tourists, and I was glad to leave.

After breakfast, I managed to fill my days mainly at home in the apartment I rented. I read voraciously, both books purchased from the one bookshop that stocked English language books and books that my mother posted to me, mostly on spiritual subjects. I practiced yoga and freestyle dance and wrote copious numbers of letters to various people (Mum received a 9-10 page hand-written letter every week with my progress – this was before the days of emails and the internet).

Egyptians are amazingly hospitable, and I was frequently invited to visit friends, including shop owners, who loved to chat over cups of tea. I met other tourists and joined them on adventures. The Egyptian afternoon ritual of a siesta following lunch became part of my routine.

I never tired of photographing the brilliant sunsets over the Nile River that drew me most evenings. This was before the era of digital cameras and the locals thought I was crazy wasting film on a photo without people in it.

And after dark, Luxor came alive and the shops stayed open until late evening; the streets were filled with throngs of pedestrians, strolling.

Occasionally, I returned to the temple in the evening. At night the lighting was beautiful, highlighting the many statues and columns that dotted the site. I noticed an unusual thing about the sounds in the temple.

Egyptians love to toot their horns and the traffic is noisy, with motorcycle exhausts blaring and the hooves of horses drawing carts clattering on the hard pavement. However, as soon as I passed through the entrance to the temple grounds—which was not surrounded by any solid walls—it felt like someone had turned down the volume. The traffic sounds died away even though the cars were still clearly visible. As soon as I exited the main gates out onto the street, the volume seemed to return back to normal. Hmm, how was that possible?

When I returned to Australia, a friend handed me a book by Egyptologist and archaeologist, Schwaller de Lubicz. It was called *The Temple of Man*. In 12 years of field work he measured the dimensions of each section of the Luxor Temple and realized that the overall layout symbolized the human body. Not only that, but the layout also demonstrated the ancient Egyptians' advanced knowledge of sacred geometry and astrological alignments. He discovered that they had compressed energy lines, which resulted in a kind of force field around the temple. Could this explain why outside sounds were so muffled? I wondered if the Ancient Egyptians had created an invisible wall around the temple that actually reflected the outside sounds.

Lubicz stated that the room I had used throughout the bulk of my time there represented the third eye. He identified it as the Holy of Holies of the temple where the High Priests ventured only once a year to retrieve a sacred statue, which was carried to Karnak Temple during a special ceremony. He wrote that the energy inside that room was so high, even today, that no one could spend more than a few minutes inside. What?! I had spent many hours in that room over an eight-month period! But I had to acknowledge that the room did have magical qualities.

During those deep meditations, I had had visions and insights. Symbolic pictures would come to me, helping me understand metaphysical and spiritual concepts in flashes of insight. One time, as I felt myself sink deeper and deeper into an altered state, the fear arose that maybe I wouldn't be able to return to waking consciousness and I pulled myself back from what seemed like an abyss.

I believe that bathing in these powerful energies over such a long period of time changed my frequency, my vibratory rate. This became evident when I visited Karnak Temple just before leaving Luxor. During a visit eight months earlier, the famous Great Hypostyle Hall— with its 134 giant columns—had felt very intimidating. The energies I sensed while walking amongst this forest of giant pillars had agitated and disturbed me greatly. I met some other tourists who were sensitive to energy, and they reported feeling the same way about the Great Hall.

I had decided never to enter that hall again. However, near the end of my writing trip a tourist I met persuaded me to accompany him to Karnak Temple as he didn't want to go alone. With slight trepidation, I entered the Great Hypostyle Hall and was shocked to feel a beautiful and powerful energy. I felt uplifted and expanded, elevated. It dawned on me that the change was in me! My vibration now resonated with the space whereas before, my energy had somehow clashed with the exalted energies of the Great Hall. When I returned to Australia my sister said she felt I was a different person.

What about the book? I couldn't get started. I didn't even know what the subject matter was supposed to be. No inspiration came, even during my deepest meditations. I began to journal about what was preventing the book from manifesting.

I poured my soul onto the pages—all the clashes I had ever had with parents, siblings, and people I had met on my travels, including some in Luxor. I poured out all of the pain of my marriage, which had ended five years earlier. My ex-husband was rejecting and humiliating me by the end of our time together, yet I was also grateful for the role he had played in extracting me from a fanatical religious group in which I had found myself. Out it all flowed onto the pages with sudden insights and understandings of what I had gained from being in the religious group and how I had expanded and grown during my marriage.

I poured out fears and emotions that I had never allowed myself to express. Everything I had bottled up inside was spewed onto the pages as I waited for the inspiration to come to write the book. I tried automatic writing but that didn't work. Maybe I needed to delve into yet another unhealed part of me before I could start?

A Child Appeared

Near the end of that eight months, a child appeared in my meditations. "Hurry up, I want to be born!" The child came several times, always with the same message, "Hurry up, I want to be born!"

"Who is the father?" I asked. There was no reply.

Once the hot weather started in earnest, I began to realize that maybe there was no book. Maybe this was some Divine plan to make me spend the time dredging through my life, sorting it out, healing. Without the book as a prize in the distance, I never would have dedicated eight months to taking this inner journey. In retrospect this time was preparing me for what lay ahead after birthing this impatient child.

Not only did my vibratory rate change but it was also as if I underwent a kind of initiation in Luxor Temple.

The advantage of travelling alone for so long in cultures so different from my own was that no one I met had any preconceived ideas and expectations about who I was and how I should behave. This liberated me to fully discover myself and step into who I truly was.

After a lifetime of trying to please others and not actually knowing what pleased me, by the end of my journeys I had seemingly reinvented myself. In reality, I had gained self-knowledge for the first time. This was a great help later as I navigated the world of disability and uncovered the best way forward for Lucy and me.

I arrived back in Melbourne after my travels feeling disoriented. This was not my place anymore, nor was Darwin, where I had spent the few years prior to travelling the world with my backpack. Feeling so different in myself, I couldn't just pick up where I had left off before. Through a series of circumstances, I found myself in Byron Bay, famous for its surf beaches, hippies, healers, musicians, and artists.

This felt like home. I started volunteering my time at the Byron Environment Centre, a not-for-profit organization educating and promoting anything to do with protecting the environment.

I became very attracted to one of the other volunteers, Hal. He was a passionate activist as well as a healer who did Zen Shiatsu and energy work. Soon we became romantically involved and I fell deeply in love.

I found work in the Department of Agriculture laboratory in Lismore 50 kilometers (about 31 miles) away. Qualified chemistry graduates like me were hard to find in that area. The working hours were very long, with 12-hour days the standard fare, and my responsibilities included working every second weekend due to an agricultural emergency so there was very little free time to spend with Hal. But my feelings for him continued to grow, even though he wanted an "open relationship" in which we would both have additional sexual partners. I reluctantly agreed just because I wanted to be with him. I had deeper feelings for him than I had ever had for my ex-husband. Maybe the healing I had done in Egypt allowed me to be more open and vulnerable in a relationship?

My body couldn't seem to tolerate the contraceptive pill even though it had never been a problem throughout my marriage. Hal said he would take responsibility. And that is how Lucy incarnated, without it being a conscious decision on my part. In fact, I had forgotten about that impatient child but as soon as I discovered that I was pregnant, I had the overwhelming sense that this was an old friend coming to be with me again.

At 37 years of age, I had resigned myself to never being a mother, so I was ecstatic when I discovered I was expecting. During my first marriage in my twenties, I had desperately wanted to start a family, but my husband had kept wanting to put it off for another year, then another. By the time we separated, I had knitted 20 baby outfits, some with Fair Isle patterns, others with intricate lace patterns, and some in rainbow colors.

I fussed over everyone else's babies, offering to babysit or take them for walks in their stroller. I cuddled any baby I could find. I fantasized about being a mum, what I would do, how it would be.

When I informed Hal that I was pregnant, he flatly replied that he would never be able to feel the same about me again. After my initial shock, I told myself he just needed time, but he urged me to terminate the pregnancy. Although I have always supported the right of a woman to choose, I always knew that I would never be able to do such a thing. My connection to this child was very strong, right from the start.

Giving Hal more time wasn't going to make a difference: he ended our relationship the night I told him I was pregnant. This felt devastating. I was on my own.

A few weeks later, on Christmas Day in 1995, I hit an all-time low when I learned that Hal had found a new girlfriend. Wracked with guilt that I was selfishly bringing a child into the world when the baby's own father didn't want it, I seriously considered terminating the pregnancy. But as I looked at my tear-stained face in the bathroom mirror I felt Lucy's presence descend upon me, so full of love, so powerful, supporting me to make the decision to move forward, fearlessly, courageously, towards becoming a sole parent.

After that evening, I never again considered the alternative. I would do everything in my power to make the best of the situation. During the pregnancy, Lucy communicated with me frequently. I was determined to be as prepared as possible to become the best mother I could be. I joined a pregnancy support group run by some homebirth midwives. They had a library of books on parenting which I read voraciously. I learned that the fetus can be affected by the mother's emotional state so when feelings of anger towards Hal surfaced, I made sure to release them as soon as possible, punching pillows, howling out my anger and grief.

I ate healthy food and went to Tai Chi classes, but as the chi moved around my body, it released a lot of grief and I ended up crying after each class.

Eventually, I stopped attending. I went to a special yoga class for expectant mothers, and I attended birth preparation classes, although I was the only one without a partner.

I chose a doctor specializing in natural childbirth who operated out of a birthing center at a small local hospital. I employed a homebirth midwife/Reiki Master to be my support person during the labor. We had met volunteering at the Environment Centre, and she was a beautiful and kind soul.

However, I decided not to attempt a homebirth; the birthing center would be natural enough, a good compromise.

The midwife was also a rebirthing practitioner and she explained that anyone who had had a traumatic birth needed to clear that in order to prevent a repeat during their labor. My own birth had been very traumatic; both my mother and I had almost died during the prolonged labor of 72 hours.

In order to create the best outcome for my child, the midwife took me through the rebirthing process which involved breath work and having to squeeze my way out of an improvised birth canal.

I felt very nurtured and cared for and I'm glad I went through the process.

Lucy was helping me to heal from my own childhood trauma as I was preparing to welcome her into the world, another powerful lesson.

Chapter 3

Preparing for the Birth

All through the pregnancy I prepared myself in every way possible and I felt that Lucy guided me to meet the right people in order to do so.

The library of books held at the pregnancy support group I attended was extensive and I borrowed many books about childbirth and parenting, a lot of them focusing on natural and alternative ways to give birth and raise children.

The two home birth midwives who ran the group facilitated wonderful discussions on what was most natural. It struck me that native cultures that have not medicalized birth were a great guide for us to follow. All over Africa and in parts of Asia, children are carried by their mothers in slings or tied to their mother's back, so I bought a sling and ended up carrying Lucy for the first five months, not using a stroller or pram once.

The book that had the biggest impact on me was called *The Aware Baby*, by Aletha Solter. It claimed to "present novice parents with a complete understanding of their baby's emotional needs from conception to two-and-a-half years of age."

Solter had a very different take on why babies cry and how best to respond. The idea was that babies cry to express their frustration and if we patiently listen to them as they express, it allows the frustration to be released.

When we try to stop them from crying by soothing them too soon, the unexpressed frustration can be suppressed and later explode as a temper tantrum. The author explained that our need to pacify the infant, rather than allow them to vent their frustration, is because their crying triggers all of our own unexpressed emotions from when we were also pacified too soon.

The book included research that indicated that if presented with a range of healthy foods and allowed to choose, a toddler would naturally choose a well-balanced diet. At times of peak growth, it might choose more protein rich foods, at other times when it required more energy it might choose more carbohydrates.

The underlying principle was that all babies are born with innate intelligence, and they will make good decisions if empowered to make their own choices. However, the best way to help them feel empowered was to offer them two choices, rather than giving them open choices with questions such as "what do you want to do now?"

The book also suggested discipline be handled very differently from how I had been raised and what I had believed. I was determined to put into practice the strategies Solter suggested. It all resonated with me and made logical sense. I, too, believed a child is born with innate intelligence; they were not blank slates needing to be filled with knowledge.

Interestingly, as I read this book and several others about strategies for child rearing, I received messages or "knowings" during journaling sessions that indicated none of the knowledge I was acquiring would apply to my child.

My child would be different, special in some way. I was mystified by this information. Was I going to give birth to some kind of child prodigy? A genius? I also received a message that the child's name should mean light. I was convinced I was having a boy because I could sense that this old friend was a male. I had many baby dreams and in every dream the baby was a boy. I scoured the name books for boys' names that meant light, but I didn't like any of them. Lucas, Luke, Aaron, Lucifer, Rupert, Egbert. In one vivid dream I was told to name the baby Anwar! An Arabic name? No, I absolutely would not! But when I looked it up, I found that Anwar means light in Arabic.

Two weeks before the due date my mum arrived, to help me during and after the birth. My relationship with my mum has always had its ups and downs. After growing up with a tyrant of a mother herself, she escaped into marriage with my father, only to end up feeling victimized by him. She blamed him for virtually everything that happened after that. From a young age I recall that I often felt responsible for caring for her, as she presented herself as such a helpless victim. Yet, regardless of that, we both underwent spiritual awakenings simultaneously when we went on a holiday together after I separated from my first husband. Coincidentally, we each took along a copy of the life-changing book, "Seth Speaks" by Jane Roberts. We read it in tandem and spent hours discussing the mind-blowing concepts it contained. My mother went on to devour many spiritual books and she could quote them to people, yet she had a hard time putting any of their wisdom into practice in her own life. She was a natural psychic and developed her own energy healing technique, sending energy from her hands. Even though she could trigger me into frustration very easily, there was a lot of love between us, and she was always there when I really needed her.

I Was Going to Have a Girl

Here she was now, dangling her pendulum over my belly and watching the direction it swung, which was clockwise. I was definitely going to have a girl. She had never been wrong using this method before, she told me. She insisted I needed girl's names, just in case. I chose Lucy (from the Latin) and Ellen, a derivation of the Greek name Helen. Both names mean light.

I was grateful to my mother when, astounded, I gave birth to a girl. Even after she was born, for the first couple of months, I sometimes forgot that Lucy was a girl, so strong was my sense that she was supposed to be a boy.

I was delighted at having a daughter. As a sole parent, I thought it would be easier to raise a girl than a boy who had no male role model and I relished the thought of doing feminine things together.

After all my reading I became convinced that bonding was essential for a baby. It's referred to as attachment. Babies do best when they have a consistent caretaker to whom they can attach, so my plan was to be a stay-at-home mum for the first two years, the most important time for this process.

It would mean relying on government benefits as my savings were insufficient and this engendered a lot of guilt. Not only was I selfishly bringing a child into the world whose father didn't want it, but I would be using taxpayers' money to raise it. However, my desire to give my child the best start in life overcame my guilt.

I had imagined that after the birth, when Hal comprehended that I was fully willing to be a sole parent, he might be interested in spending some time with our child, free of any commitments. I fantasized that he would go on occasional outings and do fun things with her. It was not to be.

His explanation was that he had been traumatized by his experience with his ex-wife. They had four children and to make ends meet, he was working two full-time jobs. His version of events was that his wife had been lonely in their marriage and had found a lover. When he discovered this, he felt completely betrayed and never recovered. Even though my situation was completely different, he claimed it triggered old painful memories. I perceived him as cowardly.

The reality was that only once did he agree to stay with Lucy when she was a baby, and this was when I had a dental appointment.

Before her first birthday, he left Byron Bay and returned to Sydney, his birthplace. He came to visit her once when she was four years old and, amazingly, he also attended her funeral.

Fortunately, my friend Jain did step in to act as a surrogate father for Lucy. He was a mathematician and a sacred geometry expert, and he was like a brother to me.

The first time we met he had been teaching a magic squares workshop in a garden at a retreat center and he had been dressed in a colorful costume complete with a Leonardo da Vinci-style hat and long dreadlocks.

He had a flipchart sewn from satin appliqué, rather than paper and a pen. I was captivated by his eccentric personality and teaching methods.

He asked for nine volunteers, so I quickly raised my hand. He numbered us off from one to nine, and we stood where instructed on a square 3-meter x 3-meter grid (about 10' x 10'). Each of us represented a number in the layout of a magic square; all columns, all rows, and both diagonals added up to the number 15.

Next, he handed us a long red string and we passed it between all nine of us as if connecting dots on paper, one to nine, the string crisscrossing amongst us.

An interesting pattern was formed called a yantra, a mystical diagram according to ancient Indian religions. If this pattern were to be drawn on paper, then the paper rotated 90° and the same pattern overlaid on the initial yantra and rotated two more times, a beautiful mandala design would emerge. If only I could have taught like this, the children would have been much more engaged.

After the presentation, I approached Jain to chat some more. He was delighted to meet a fellow math teacher and we discussed sacred geometry, educational methods, and our philosophies of life, which were remarkably similar. And so, our friendship began.

After falling pregnant, when I next saw Jain, he said that he had received a kind of psychic message that he was very connected to my baby and believed he would be playing a part in the child's life. How exciting!

Before Lucy was born, I read several of Dervla Murphy's wonderful travel books. My favorite was *Eight Feet in the Andes*, where the author travels with her nine-year-old daughter and a mule across the mountains in Peru.

I had wonderful images of continuing my adventure travels with my child in tow. How different the reality was.

Travelling on a plane with a long legged four-year-old with a soiled diaper and being told that she could only be changed inside the toilet using the pulldown change table designed for infants, taxed all my ingenuity and fortitude. It was enough to put me off air travel with her for good.

I had images of walks along the beach, hand-in-hand with my child. As it turns out, wheelchairs containing heavy children are not designed to plough through soft sand in order to get to the firm sand at the water's edge. Believe me, I tried. Even hauling the chair backwards didn't work.

I imagined walking my child to the nearby school each day. Instead, before we got a wheelchair van with a motorized hoist, I had to manhandle her out of her chair into a special car seat, then strain my back to get her out of the car seat and back into the wheelchair once we reached the school.

I imagined chatting with my child, sharing our hopes and dreams. In reality, Lucy was never able to speak.

Preparing for my daughter's birth was a wonderful if intimidating project for me and I was committed to becoming the best mother I could be. Little did I know that none of my preparations could possibly ready me for the parenting adventure that was to unfold on the other side of birth.

What awaited me was going to test me beyond the limits of my capabilities. And no amount of planning could have prepared me for the path ahead.

Chapter 4

The Child Who Didn't Die

It was a shock to be told that my baby was not going to make it.

All through the pregnancy my intention had been to give birth as naturally as possible. My birth plan included playing music by Mozart throughout the birthing process, refusing all drugs, and forgoing all interventions such as breaking the amniotic sac, undergoing an episiotomy, and the use of forceps. I wanted to allow the umbilical cord to stop pulsing before it was cut. The lights would be low, and the baby was to be immediately placed on my chest to bond and suckle.

I chose a local GP (general practitioner) who advocated natural childbirth. He believed in waiting till the baby decided it was time to arrive. So, we waited, and waited. Each week that I was overdue, he monitored the fetal heartbeat...no problems, he would say. Just wait some more.

My mother had come to support me during the birth, so we were forced to extend her return date several times as the weeks kept passing with no result. My friend the home-birth midwife and Reiki Master invited me over several times during the last months of the pregnancy so that she could telepathically tune into the baby. Each time, she reported that all was well, just follow the doctor's advice and wait. With her fetal heart monitor, we listened to the heartbeat. It was strong and regular, indicating that the baby was not stressed.

I finally went into labor three weeks after my due date. Arriving at the birthing unit, my blood pressure was found to be dangerously high, indicating a condition known as pre-eclampsia. No amount of Reiki, meditation, or slow breathing could reduce it. There was no option but to send me to a larger hospital with an obstetrician and a pediatrician.

My first lesson had been patience. My next lesson was to be flexible. To get to the hospital required a 40-minute ambulance journey along a winding road. I don't normally experience motion sickness, but it took all my willpower not to vomit as I lay on the gurney in labor as the ambulance twisted and turned our way to the hospital.

My blood pressure reading was dangerously high upon arrival, so drugs were the only solution and I was given pethidine. "There goes the drug-free birthing plan!" I thought. Then I had the premature urge to push before I was fully dilated, and hospital staff told me I must resist at all costs or risk tearing my cervix.

The instructor in my birthing classes had trained me to make a low sound with each contraction and each urge to push but my midwife told me instead to make a high sound and imagine myself in a high place, like a mountain top, while I fought the powerful urge to bear down.

The baby wanted to come out, but I wasn't dilating. Hour after hour, I imagined myself on mountain tops in every country I had visited during my world travels. As I said earlier, I love mountains and had trekked up many during my back-packing adventures. I recalled Mount Kilimanjaro in Kenya, the Andes in Peru and Bolivia, volcanos in Chile and Argentina, the Annapurna Range in Nepal, the Swiss Alps.

Closer to home, I recalled visits to the Snowy Mountains in Australia, Uluru....it was quite fun recalling all my adventures and it did help me resist the urge to push, but as the hours passed, I ran out of places I had visited and then started imagining mountains that I had never visited, still making my high sounds, still using all my strength to resist the urge to bear down and push the baby out.

It was determined that I had "incoordinate" contractions. The muscles were not working together and were ineffective at dilating my cervix, so more drugs were called for and, finally, I started to dilate. But I was still required to resist the urge to push. After 12 hours of resisting the urge, I gave up and agreed to an epidural, which anesthetized the muscles that wanted to push.

The doctors then insisted on cutting the amniotic sack in which my baby was encased to release the amniotic fluid in which she was floating, a procedure referred to as "breaking the waters." Instead of the clear fluid medical staff expected, what emerged was a light brown "mud." I had no idea of the significance of this at the time, but soon the room began to fill with doctors, nurses, student doctors, and student nurses. About a dozen medical staff were crowded into the delivery room to watch the drama unfolding.

The natural birthing advocates I had consulted suggested I not lie on my back during labor because it is said to hamper the process but once the epidural had paralyzed my legs, lying on my side required my midwife to hold my leg up. At my own birth, I had been delivered with forceps and this had led to life-long problems with my neck and right ear, so I refused to let the doctors use forceps now. Instead, they insisted on a suction device to extract the baby's head.

Finally, she was out but my dream of resting my little baby on my abdomen and waiting for the umbilical cord to stop pulsing before it was cut evaporated as medical staff cut the cord immediately, brought her muddied body towards me for a split-second view and then whisked her off to the Intensive Care Unit (ICU) and inserted a tube down her throat to help her breathe.

This hospital didn't have a ventilating machine, so the nurses took turns hand pumping the air into her tiny lungs for a few hours until a helicopter arrived with a "retrieval team" from Mater Mothers' Hospital in Brisbane. She was to be air lifted to their Neonatal Intensive Care Unit (NICU). Couldn't I accompany Lucy in the helicopter, too? I asked. There was no room for me. I was left behind with two polaroid photos of her as consolation. I desperately wanted to go with them. I needed to be with my baby, to bond with her. How could this be happening?

I was sent to a four-bed ward with three other mothers who were cooing over their new-born babies. My two photos were propped up on the bedside table and I felt numb. Nothing had gone to plan, nothing. And no one told me the significance of what had just happened. I assumed my baby just needed some special help, then all would be well the next day and I could take her home...

Mater Mothers' Hospital

The next morning, my midwife friend drove Mum and me to Mater Mothers' Hospital in Brisbane, a journey of about 90 minutes. We were all joking and optimistic. We stopped for a delicious lunch before arriving at the hospital.

I was excited at the prospect of finally cradling my daughter, Lucy Ellen, in my arms. But a huge shock awaited me.

Feeling intimidated by the noises and the sights, I followed the nurse who guided me to Lucy. She was right at the end of the room, and I had to walk past about 10 other babies, some as tiny as my outstretched palm, to get to her. She was lying in a small crib with no sides, and she was naked except for a diaper and a little pink knitted beany on her head.

Lucy was hooked up to numerous machines with tubes and wires that were monitoring her vital signs and helping her breathe and eat. Along the wall was the row of machines keeping her alive, some beeping, some with flashing lights. I was totally unprepared for this surreal scene, and I felt apprehensive and overwhelmed.

A serious-looking doctor explained the gravity of the situation. The light colored "mud" in which she had been born indicated massive trauma in the womb, probably one or two months prior to birth. Known as meconium, it is a bowel motion that a fetus passes when under huge stress. It is usually black in color when it is fresh. The fact that it was light brown indicated it was old.

A CT scan and arterial studies of Lucy's brain showed a massive brain injury caused by a lack of oxygen (reason unknown) and there was a lot of swelling in the brain. There was no hope for her. I just needed to sign a consent form to give doctors permission to switch off the life-support system the following morning at 10:00 a.m. No explanation was given as to why it would be done at 10:00 a.m. the next morning but maybe the doctor thought it would help me to have one last evening with her.

My mind was reeling. I was being told to agree to letting my daughter die. Couldn't we at least wait till someone could locate her father and let him come and see her first? No, they couldn't wait, I needed to sign the form now, so that the next morning at 10:00 a.m. the ventilator could be switched off. Still feeling numb, I signed the form, believing I had no other choice.

Lucy's head was so swollen that the pressure had suppressed all the natural reflexes of a new-born. There was no grasping action when I touched her palm, and no sucking action; there was no kicking or any other movement at all. Lucy's eyes were shut, and it looked as if she were in a coma. Perhaps she was, I am not sure.

The nurses in the NICU were marvelous. They suggested I do a "kangaroo cuddle" where I opened my shirt and held her against my chest, skin to skin. It has been shown to help infants recover quicker from trauma. It was a challenge to arrange the tubes and wires correctly so we could achieve this without disconnecting anything, but the nurse who assisted was patient with me. Lucy was motionless, but warm against my skin.

How does one prepare mentally for switching off the life-support system of their new-born baby? The staff fed Lucy with formula through a tube in her nose that passed into her stomach. Did I want to express some breast milk to use instead of formula? "What was the point?" I asked myself. Of course, I had planned to breast feed my baby. It was in my birthing plan. But not like this, through a tube, and not for less than one day.

In self-defense, I began to withdraw. I didn't want to bond with a child that I was going to lose the next day, so I went back to the room they had assigned me, amongst all the new mothers and their babies, and tried to rest, but sleep would not come. How could I rest as my mind went over and over the events of the last 24 hours, trying to make sense of them? Here were mothers with their babies next to them, oblivious to my inner turmoil.

My bedside phone rang. It was a nurse from NICU. "Why are you not here with your baby?" she asked me. "She needs you here." Guilt-ridden and emotionally exhausted, I dragged myself there. It was midnight, and no other parents were around. I decided to send Lucy some Reiki. What else could I do for her? I gently rested my palms over the cables and tubes connecting her to life and sent healing energy to her.

At one point, I placed my finger on her tiny palm and spoke to her. I told her that if she wanted to live, then I would always be there for her, no matter what happened. Unbelievably, her little hand closed around my finger. There was no other movement, just her hand briefly holding my finger in answer.

After several more hours of Reiki and talking to her, I went back to bed and tried to prepare for the momentous morning ahead. I arrived in the NICU for 10:00 a.m. to find the staff had dressed Lucy in a pretty pink gown, open at the sides where the tubes were located. Then they began to remove all the tubes and wires. As I watched the nurse work to remove the wires and finally the ventilator tube from her throat, the inner pain I felt was excruciating. Once the ventilator was removed, I could finally see her pretty face properly. Did I want to hold her until she stopped breathing, the nurse asked me? Yes, please. I held her and rocked her gently and waited. My arms began to ache with holding her so long and still she breathed. She would stop for a little while and her lips would start to turn blue; then she would start to breathe again and her lips would become pink.

Was there somewhere that I could lay down with her while I waited? Staff members kindly arranged for me to use a small room with a bed that was reserved for parents of premature babies who came for overnight visits. I decided to dress her up in her "going home" outfit that I had hand-knitted with loving care. At least it could get one use. It felt like dressing a doll. She was motionless and had not yet uttered a single cry. Her lips alternated between pink and blue, pink and blue as she would stop breathing and then spontaneously start again.

Four hours later, the pediatrician who had insisted I sign the consent form so quickly came to the small room. "She is still breathing? Well, we can't let her starve to death, can we? We will commence tube feeding."

I watched as the nurse skillfully slipped a naso-gastric tube through Lucy's nose and into her stomach. She taught me how to use a syringe to slowly trickle formula into her stomach. Later, a kindly nurse suggested we give her a bath, to finally clean off the residual mud-like meconium that still adhered to Lucy's skin. She recorded a video of me awkwardly handling my motionless baby and bathing her in the little tub.

Lismore Base Hospital

The next day, Lucy was still breathing so it was decided that we should be relocated to yet another hospital, Lismore Base Hospital, closer to home, where they had a palliative care unit. This was our fourth hospital in three days. Was this some kind of record? We travelled in a car ambulance, and this time I was allowed to travel with my baby. The driver said he had never transported a silent baby before!

On arrival, we were introduced to a new set of medical staff members and a social worker specializing in Stillbirths and Neonatal Death Support (SANDS). His name was Angel. I will never forget that name. He let Mum and me talk through all that had happened so far. I guess it was helpful. The new pediatrician explained that occasionally these children can last a few days or even weeks before they stop breathing, so if she was still alive after a week, we could take her home.

It felt like being in limbo, a kind of time warp, waiting for the inevitable but with no idea when that would occur. Part of me was preparing for the worst, part of me was still hopeful that things could turn around. On the sixth day of our stay in that hospital, Mum offered to send some healing energy to Lucy's head, which was still very swollen. The protocol she used was her own invention, and it was similar to Reiki. Mum spent almost two hours directing energy at Lucy's brain. Up until this time, Lucy had not responded in any way.

However, she suddenly started sucking her clenched fist, the first reflex to appear. We excitedly called the nurse to look and soon the pediatrician arrived. He noted that the swelling in her head was subsiding and predicted that other reflexes would soon start to manifest. He suggested that we offer her a bottle and when she became too tired to suck, we could pour the remaining formula through the naso-gastric tube into her stomach. Rather than discharging us the next day as originally planned, the doctor encouraged us to stay longer and see how bottle feeding progressed. As predicted, other reflexes began to appear: the startle (Moro) reflex, the palm-gripping reflex, and then on day nine, while I was bathing her, Lucy uttered her first cry—a short, loud yell—before promptly falling asleep in the bath.

Gradually, the sucking improved until she could finish a whole bottle before tiring herself out. It was time to remove the feeding tube and go home. Lucy was exceeding all expectations, but the prognosis was still grim. The doctor told me she would eventually stop breathing.

However, at the urging of my midwife friend, I decided to try breastfeeding. After being introduced to the breast, Lucy refused the bottle!

We were referred to another pediatrician in private practice and he was pessimistic about breastfeeding. How could we monitor how much she consumed? But I was adamant. He insisted on weekly visits to monitor her weight gain, convinced that it would not increase at an acceptable rate. However, defying the odds, Lucy thrived and became chubby. Finally, he conceded that breastfeeding was working and reduced the visits to once a month. But he insisted that she would always be small for her age. (Hmmm. With two tall parents, I wasn't so sure about that).

Ever since the momentous healing from my Mum at nine days of age, Lucy's breathing had been fine, and there had been no more blue lip episodes. She had exceeded expectations and defied all of the doctors' predictions. She appeared to be thriving.

However, I was told that with the degree of damage she had sustained to her brain, she could still stop breathing at any time. I was conflicted. Each prognosis she defied excited me and gave me hope, but I was also preparing myself for the worst.

A friend suggested that I change pediatricians and find one who would be more open-minded about Lucy's seemingly miraculous improvement.

Looking back, I'm not sure why I felt so guilty abandoning the first pediatrician, even though he had continued to be so pessimistic. I changed to a young, kindly, and open-minded doctor who was as excited as I was at every unexpected improvement. There was a moment of embarrassment when I crossed paths with the old doctor one day at the hospital and he asked why we hadn't come to see him lately. I sheepishly told him I was now seeing the other pediatrician—as there were only two choices in Lismore, he knew exactly who that was. But I learned that it was important for me to choose positive people who took the time to listen to what I had to say and encouraged me.

Many months later, at one of Lucy's checkups, the newer pediatrician asked me, "Do you think your daughter knows what is going on?" He explained that the kind of brain damage Lucy had affects the parts of the brain responsible for muscle movement—the motor cortex and the cerebellum—and it may or may not have affected the intellectual parts of her brain also.

I told him that I believed she was fully aware of what was going on. How did I know she was fully aware of what was going on? Her communications with me were very subtle as I carefully observed every reaction to the world around her, the way she responded to people, snuggling into some, leaning away from others. She was sensitive to where we were and what was happening, and I could sense that she was engaged with the world. The doctor sighed and said that communication with her would become our biggest challenge.

At the time, I did not pay much attention to what he said. Lucy was still less than a year old and I couldn't think far ahead, especially when I was still being told she would not survive long.

However, the doctor was right. One of the biggest challenges for me was to interpret her cries and other sounds and try to fulfil her needs.

Before Lucy's birth, I had received clear psychic or telepathic communication from her. One day when I had been six months pregnant, I was sitting on a beach watching the sunset when I received a clear message from her that she wanted her father to place his hands on my belly and tune in to her; she had a message for him. My first response was that I had no idea where Hal was. We hardly ever crossed paths by then. He might not have been in Byron Bay that day, for all I knew. Yet I received a clear message from Lucy that he was alone at the Environment Centre. Sure enough, she was right.

Feeling apprehensive about even speaking with him, let alone passing this unconventional message along, I was surprised when he agreed to Lucy's request. He came to my home and as I lay down, he placed his hands on my belly to have some silent communication with her. I never learned what it was about.

After her dramatic entrance into the world, I lost my telepathic connection to Lucy. Having subsequently learned about the autonomic nervous system, "fight and flight," and "rest and digest" modes, I can see that for most of her life I was stuck in "fight and flight" mode, reacting to one seeming disaster after another, cut off from deep intuition and telepathic communication.

Instead, I became super tuned to observing her various sounds and cries, guessing their meaning. Was she in pain? Did she want to be moved to a different position? Did she want to listen to some music? What type of music? Trial and error, trial, and error.

Chapter 5

Life with Lucy

Having embraced life, Lucy grew. And much as I was grateful for my daughter's determination to embrace life, struggle became a key ingredient in our days.

Nothing ever went "according to plan" in Lucy's life. We were constantly challenged by surprise medical issues that came with recommended interventions.

I resisted much of what we were told to do, at least in the beginning, as I had a strong faith in complementary therapies, which I explored with Lucy throughout her life. Some of these therapies were more successful than others and over time I began to value conventional treatments, as many of them proved to enhance Lucy's quality of life, if not keep her alive.

Lucy's physical development went like this:

6 months: Lucy was diagnosed with cerebral palsy

10 months: Lucy was diagnosed with epilepsy

15 months: A gastrostomy tube was inserted.

18 months: We started early intervention services including physiotherapy, occupational therapy, and speech therapy.

Two years:	Lucy's cortical vision impairment was diagnosed.
	Lucy received her first standing frame to facilitate putting weight on her legs each day.
Three years:	She was fitted with her first pair of ankle-foot orthoses (AFOs) which strapped her feet in a flexed position to prevent her from excessively pointing her toes, which would have led to shortening of the calf muscle. With the AFOs, we attempted to help her to take steps while supporting her body, but she had great difficulty putting each foot forward, although she tried very hard.
Four years:	Precocious puberty was triggered (more about that later).
	Lucy started horseback riding with Riding for the Disabled (RDA).
Five years:	Lucy's first surgery for her dislocated hips (she spent four weeks thereafter in a broomstick plaster cast).
	She started school, two days per week at the local primary school and three days per week at the specialist school for children with disabilities.

Six years:	Major surgery to reconstruct her hips.
	The Make-A-Wish Foundation sent us to the theme parks in Queensland.

After age six, Lucy needed no more major surgery, but she continued with regular physiotherapy, occupational therapy, and speech therapy at the specialist school for the remainder of her life. As she aged, she outgrew several wheelchairs, standing frames and pairs of AFOs. Extensive therapy sessions were not able to achieve any real advancements in her physical skills. However, these therapies helped to prevent further problems from occurring, particularly with her hips.

It didn't take me long to realize it was imperative that we develop a stable routine to counterbalance the inevitable medical crises that arose. Once Lucy was old enough to attend special schools part-time our typical daily routine on non-school days would start at about 7:00 a.m. when Lucy would call me to get her up. After first changing her diaper and hoisting her out of the bed and into her wheelchair, I would wheel her to the living room, and she would have her tube feed breakfast. The breakfast feed also included epilepsy meds when she needed them.

After breakfast, every second day, I would take her back to the bedroom and after hoisting her onto the bed, I would administer a tube of laxative into the rectum to stimulate a bowel movement if she hadn't had one unassisted. During the last few years of her life, she almost always needed assistance to initiate a bowel movement. Then I would hoist her onto the toilet commode and strap her in, and while waiting for a result, I would carefully wash the feeding tubes from breakfast. This needed to be done thoroughly with hot soapy water to minimize any bacterial build up in the tube. It wasn't advisable to put any disinfectant into the tubes in case some inadvertently went into her stomach during the next feed. Initially, the dietician gave us one set of tubes per week. But when we realized that Lucy would develop an upset tummy and vomit consistently on the sixth day the dietician suggested changing the tubes every third or fourth day, and this problem went away.

Next, it was time to place her in her standing frame for at least an hour to help strengthen her legs. And by mid-morning it was time for some water to be administered down the tube, with 30 milliliters (about one ounce) of prune juice added to help the bowels. Before lunch, I placed Lucy in her saddle chair and she could look at a book with vision patterns on it while I played some music, or we would cuddle on the sofa.

A Wheelchair-Friendly Track

Lunch was a repeat of breakfast and once the tubes were washed, we often went for a drive. I would load her into our van using the wheelchair hoist and then strap the wheelchair down to the tracks in the floor of the van. We would head out to do some shopping or take a walk. My favorite destination was Lake Daylesford. We went there at least once a week and I would push Lucy around the perimeter of the lake on a gravel track that was, thankfully, wheelchair friendly. The only steep incline had asphalt on the path, making it easy to push her up the hill. I would push her chair out onto one of the jetties to look at the ducks who would swim over hoping for some food. It was wonderful in Spring when little flocks of ducklings would swim after their mothers. I loved the sight of the duck tails as they bobbed their heads down into the water to feed. A rarer sight was a single family of black swans that had made Lake Daylesford their home. In spring, the parents would swim on either side of the baby cygnets— usually there were just two of them. In the warmer months, the brightly colored peddle boats would splash their way around the lake, with laughing children or romantic couples gently peddling their way over the smooth surface. Lucy enjoyed being outdoors in the fresh air, and the exercise and peaceful atmosphere at the lake always lifted my spirits.

I would take the short feeding tube with us so I could administer Lucy's afternoon water on our outings. Usually, she was dressed in a warm jacket with a beany on her head and sheepskin moccasins on her feet to keep them warm. Not being able to run around, she easily became chilled (especially her feet and lower legs) and for most of the year, the climate in Daylesford was quite cool, since it was located in the Central Highlands of Victoria. In winter, I wrapped blankets around her as well.

At dinner time, we repeated the feeding routine and then it was bath time. Undressing Lucy on the bed, I used the bath sling (a special mesh sling) to hoist her into a warm bath which ensured her feet and lower legs warmed up if they had happened to become too cool. I kept a heater on in the bedroom that was set to a very warm temperature during her bath times, just to make sure she didn't cool down afterwards.

Once she was dry, I rolled her, while she was still naked, onto her tummy to do her physio exercises and air her bottom. At this point I would sing and tell silly stories just to make the exercises more fun, but generally, she enjoyed taking the pressure off her back and bottom and was very relaxed and cheerful.

At age three Lucy had to start wearing plastic splints, specially molded to her foot shape, in order to keep her feet and ankles aligned correctly with her lower legs. These ankle foot orthoses (AFOs) covered the whole of the bottom of each foot, then went around her ankles and ended two thirds of the way up her calves. There was a strap at each ankle that needed to be done up very tightly to hold her foot at a 90° angle and to stop her stretching out her feet and pointing her toes.

Another strap was located near the top of the AFO, around her calf. Being unable to move her feet all day was one of the reasons her feet became so cold and sometimes, after one of our outings, if her feet felt too cold, I would remove the AFOs and massage them till they warmed up again. Her feet were only out of the AFOs during bathing and the post-bath exercise time; then I would strap them back on for bed.

Once Lucy was dressed in her pajamas, I would roll her onto her side and lift the railing at the side of the hospital bed she slept in and place a pillow between her back and the railing to keep her from rolling over. With a good night kiss, I left her to fall off to sleep.

Some nights, she would wake up and became very animated during the night, laughing and chatting, sometimes very loudly, as if a party were going on in her bedroom. I suspected that she had nocturnal visitors, her friends on the other side, and they were a very cheerful bunch. Sometimes her bursts of laughter made me think someone must have just cracked a great joke! Although they sometimes woke me up, these nighttime parties were a solace for me and also made me chuckle. I was concerned at how little she could meaningfully interact with her peers. She couldn't go on playdates or sleepovers with friends, but she obviously had some great friends coming to visit her. I learned from her that although her life didn't resemble other children's lives, it was still rich and meaningful. It's okay to be differently-abled; hers was not a life to be pitied. And Lucy never exhibited any self-pity.

Communicating with Lucy

When she was about three years old a caregiver identified that Lucy was using a hand signal—lifting her right hand up—to indicate "yes," or "more," or "I like that." Knowing this did make things easier for me. She never had a signal for no, however.

When she was six years old a psychic friend told me that Lucy wanted to go to Disneyland. My heart sank when Lucy excitedly lifted her arm several times in agreement. When the Make-A-Wish Foundation representatives came to visit to verify her wish, three of them sat in a row on the sofa. I explained to them her method of communication and asked her to show them that she wanted to go. No response. I asked again, nothing. I was mortified: they had driven 50 kilometers (about 31 miles) to make this home visit and Lucy was not cooperating.

Finally, after repeated attempts, they took pity on me and decided to grant her wish. However, they explained that Make-A-Wish had implemented a new policy that any child under 10 years of age could not travel to Disneyland in California but instead, would be sent to the Gold Coast in Queensland for a week to visit the Movie World, Dreamworld, and SeaWorld theme parks. This was much better for me, knowing the challenges of flying with all Lucy's gear. A two-hour flight was much more doable than a 13-hour flight to

Disneyland. After the incident with the three Make-A-Wish ladies, I noticed that Lucy didn't like "performing" on demand. She liked to communicate spontaneously. If I ever excitedly wanted to show off her skills, she would not cooperate.

Our Make-A-Wish trip to the Gold Coast turned out to be a big adventure. I had insisted on taking my 16-year-old nephew to help me lift Lucy on and off rides and I knew he would have a great time. Lucy's favorite ride was called the Bermuda Triangle, which was a kind of ghost train ride. The carriage was taken up a sharp incline until we were inside a fake volcano. It was very dark and there was a lot of smoke and steam, and "aliens" were visible when lights flashed on. Lucy was able to sit upright between my nephew and me in the carriage.

During the ride inside the volcano Lucy kept excitedly lifting her hand over and over, saying "I like this, more please!" We exited the volcano with our carriage rushing down a steep slope into water, making a huge splash, which she also loved. Back at the loading platform, I pleaded with the ride attendant to let us go one more time around. No, she needed to be lifted back into her chair and sent to the back of the line to wait her turn. Getting her out of her chair and into the carriage that one time was back-breaking work. I decided once was enough.

Facilitated Communication

When Lucy was four-years old, I learned about Rosemary Crossley, a communications expert, and I made an appointment for Lucy to have a session with her. Rosemary was an occupational therapist who became famous after writing a controversial book called, *Annie's Coming Out*. It was eventually turned into a film, and I was deeply moved by it.

Fresh out of training in the 1970s, Rosemary had been assigned to an institution in Melbourne back when they used to tell parents that nothing could be done with their severely disabled children and that the best option was to put them in an institution for life. Rows of cots containing mostly motionless children filled a room. They were fed and bathed but mostly just left on their own.

Rosemary wanted to know if any of them could communicate with her. She connected with a young girl named Annie McDonald, who had severe cerebral palsy. Annie was unable to sit independently and unable to communicate but Rosemary detected a sparkle in her eyes when she attempted to communicate with her. Rosemary developed a system of supporting her hand and allowing her to spell out messages by pointing at an alphabet board. She discovered that Annie was highly intelligent, simply trapped in a body that prevented her from communicating in the usual ways.

Rosemary's technique, called Facilitated Communication, allowed Annie to eventually complete a university degree and co-write the book with Rosemary.I noted that Wikipedia, notorious for discrediting all forms of alternative therapies, has the listing: "Rosemary Crossley is an Australian author and one of the first major advocates for Facilitated Communication, a scientifically discredited technique which purports to help non-verbal people communicate."[i] I felt this was poppycock.

Lucy *loved* Rosemary from the moment they met. I believe that there was a lot of telepathic communication going on as well as the facilitated communication. Rosemary used special recording devices that operated when the individual lightly touched a fist or finger to a large colorful button. Choosing two devices with differently colored buttons, Rosemary recorded "yes" on one device and "no" on the other and placed them next to each other. By supporting Lucy's wrist and relaxing the spasticity in her arm, Rosemary could ask Lucy a question and Lucy would be able to press either button in response.

I believe that the reason Wikipedia claims the method is scientifically discredited is because it takes skill and a lot of patience to give a child time to make conscious movements towards the button of their choice. An onlooker may believe that the facilitator is moving the person's arm, but I can attest that the facilitator can feel the small deliberate movements the child makes towards the button of choice. It is not a trick. However, not everyone can successfully facilitate. It needs a calm, kind, patient person who really respects the child and believes they have the mental capacity to want to communicate.

One such person was Lucy's aide at the local childcare center. She was able to master the technique, and this allowed the children and staff to ask Lucy yes/no questions. One little girl offered to do a dance for Lucy and then asked her "did you like that, Lucy?" Lucy went straight for the no button. Crestfallen, the girl did another dance. "How about this one, Lucy? Did you like that?" No. By now the little girl was distressed and the aide scolded Lucy for hurting her friend's feelings. Lucy simply burst out laughing. She was teasing the little girl!

After this incident I excitedly went to our next appointment with Lucy's speech pathologist to demonstrate Lucy's new "trick." Lucy did not seem to like this therapist. She didn't believe that Lucy had high cognitive function, so Lucy obliged her by not showing any! On this particular day Lucy completely refused to cooperate, pressing neither button no matter how much I coerced or cajoled her.

I myself had limited success with these devices. In retrospect, I don't think I was calm and patient enough to be a good facilitator because I was so stressed most of the time.

However, I knew without a doubt that Lucy was intelligent and very aware of what was going on. She laughed at jokes told by other children, which requires a level of cognitive development, imagination, and wordplay. She could read people's energies and she could let me know, via crying, if she did not like someone or did not want to be left with someone. I always respected her judgement and acted upon her communications.

Life would have been a whole lot easier if I had been able to communicate with Lucy telepathically the whole time, rather than just during the last few weeks before she passed away.

I remember one time when she cried almost continuously for about 36 hours, before I finally worked out what the problem was. I can't recall what it was now, but she was in serious pain until I solved the problem and then she relaxed. I'm sure she was just as frustrated as I was that I couldn't work out what she needed for such a long time.

I think the gift I received from the difficulty with communication is that I discovered that it is only when our mind is quiet and still that we can truly listen to another person.

It is easy for our mental chatter, worries, and fears to interfere, and allow us to presume we know what another person is trying to communicate, rather than truly listening from the heart with an open mind.

Chapter 6

Treatment for Lucy

When I was about 12 years old my mother became "a health food nut."

She researched all manner of natural therapies, preferring them to drugs. She read books about the latest health foods so my brother, sister, and I had apple cider vinegar if our stomachs were upset, raw honey instead of sugar as our only sweetener, and whole wheat bread...while all of my friends enjoyed white bread sandwiches for lunch.

My mother discovered Dr. Wilhelm Heinrich Schuessler's work on homeopathic tissue salts, so we had a full set of the 12 tissue salts in our medicine cabinet. Whatever ailment we had, she would search through the book and, based on our symptoms, select whichever remedy we needed.

By the time I was in my mid-teens, we went to a naturopath who prescribed foul-tasting herbal tinctures and we had chiropractic adjustments when needed. I learned from my chiropractor that all my ear infections in early childhood had been connected to my forceps birth: it had caused the top two cervical vertebrae to jam together and press on some nerves.

Once corrected, my ear infections stopped. This had convinced me to not allow the doctors to use forceps during my labor. As it was, they did use a suction device to pull Lucy out, so I took her to a chiropractor specializing in children to get her neck assessed and adjusted when she was only a few weeks old.

With all the grim prognoses from the doctors, I was necessarily thrust into the high-tech medical world straight after Lucy's birth. Incorporating as many natural therapies as possible into her regimen became a delicate balancing act; I didn't want to abandon medical interventions altogether. Lucy seemed to respond positively to Reiki healing: I had had first-hand evidence that it worked the night before the doctor switched off her ventilator. Mum's healing energy had managed to reduce the swelling in Lucy's head to the point where the sucking and startle reflexes had returned. Other people offered Reiki and she always responded well.

When I first observed Lucy having a seizure, I resisted telling the pediatrician. I guessed it would lead to the need for medication. But when she was about 10 months old, she had a major seizure that wouldn't stop. It was nighttime but I mustered the courage to call the pediatrician's emergency number and he immediately urged me to bring her to the base hospital in Lismore, an hour's drive through winding roads from where we were living in Byron Bay. I was frightened. Lucy seemed to be unconscious—or was she just asleep?

The drive on that dark, winding road seemed to go on forever. As soon as we reached the hospital, the pediatrician administered Valium (diazepam) rectally, explaining that it was the quickest way for the body to absorb the drug, and she was brought back to full consciousness. I sighed with relief, but at the same time, acknowledged that drugs were going to become a routine part of our lives. An EEG of her brain revealed abnormal brainwave activity caused by massive scar tissue in the brain. This had led to short circuits—seizures. All of this was the result of oxygen deprivation in utero.

The search began to determine which drug would stop her seizures, as these became quite frequent after that very big one. Untreated, a long seizure could stop her breathing with fatal consequences.

We started with the mildest drug, Epilim, which was a bright pink liquid. However, that didn't work. I learned the process of weaning her off one drug whilst slowly introducing her to another antiseizure medication. One after another, we kept looking for something that would work. Some tablets had to be cut in half and ground so I could mix them with water and Lucy could take them. No single medication was effective, so we next started experimenting with combinations, first two, then three different drugs simultaneously. Even with three drugs she still had the occasional seizure. My task was to time them.

If a seizure didn't finish in five minutes, I needed to administer the rectal Valium. This meant I needed to carry some with me at all times, just in case. When she was 14 months old Lucy was no longer able to suck and a gastrostomy tube was inserted into her stomach. This made it very easy to administer the epilepsy drugs, so that was a bonus. Sadly, the side-effects of being on so many antiseizure drugs—which act as tranquillizers—was that Lucy eventually relaxed into a perpetually drowsy state. She didn't smile or interact with me at all. At times, it felt like I was caring for a zombie. We don't realize how precious a smile of recognition from our child can be until there are none. No recognition, no feedback—that's quite soul-destroying for a parent. The only upside was that now that she had been diagnosed as having "uncontrolled epilepsy"—which is a life-threatening condition—we qualified for additional support.

Lucy had been officially diagnosed with cerebral palsy (CP) by the time she was six months old, but it had

62

not been designated as life-threatening. She had the moderately severe version known as spastic quadriplegia, which meant all four limbs were affected. Spasticity occurs when some sets of muscles are continuously activated by short circuits in the brain, but the opposing muscles are not—for example, the biceps flex the arm, and the triceps are the opposing muscle which straighten the arm. If one muscle is continuously triggered, it can become very stiff and strong, but the opposing muscle becomes very weak. So, Lucy's inner thigh muscles, the adductors, were very strong but her outer thigh muscles, the abductors, were overly weak. The constant pulling of her legs inwards led to the gradual shortening of these muscles which resulted in her hips dislocating, which was very painful.

An additional problem associated with the uncontrolled epilepsy and the possible need to administer Valium was that only qualified staff were allowed to care for her. It was challenging for me to get any type of break from caring for her 24 hours a day. Thank goodness for an organization called, "Very Special Kids" (VSK). It was set up as a charity to give parents of children with life-threatening illnesses a break from the demanding role of caregiver. Staffed around the clock by nurses and an on-call doctor, it allowed parents a chance to relax and enjoy a few days' break without worrying about our children. On my first break, when Lucy was three years old, I went to the cinema for the first time since she had been born. It was such a delight to immerse myself in the story and completely forget about my caring role for a couple of hours.

My quest for natural therapies continued throughout Lucy's life. A foot reflexologist offered to make weekly visits to our home, and she donated her services. But Lucy did not seem to like the treatments and there were no improvements in her condition, so we eventually stopped these sessions. A ray of hope came when a healer, Heather, contacted me and offered to treat Lucy for free using a new energy technique she had developed. I felt there was no harm in trying. However, at our first meeting she was confused because her experience had been with autistic children. She had erroneously been told that Lucy was autistic, and she had never tried her therapy on someone with cerebral palsy. After her initial reluctance, she decided to see what would happen, and a long-standing relationship began.

Healing Energy

Standing a few feet away from Lucy, Heather faced her open palms towards her and sent in energy. Lucy immediately responded positively, obviously enjoying the healing energy being administered. We could see some improvements in her alertness. We decided to continue the treatments once a week. The sessions lasted between one and two hours and I was impressed with Heather's dedication and perseverance. She refused all payment, so I occasionally brought her gifts and some fruit as an offering. Each week, Lucy would become animated when she knew it was time to visit Heather, especially in the car as we got closer to Heather's house when she would start vocalizing loudly and throwing up her right arm. Heather seemed to have a telepathic communication with Lucy, and they had a good relationship. One day, Heather said that she was convinced that Lucy didn't need her epilepsy medication anymore. She had not had any seizures since we had started the treatments. This was a big decision for me to make and Heather suggested I talk with the pediatrician we were seeing at the time.

I felt sure he would be against the idea. I decided to do an experiment. Using my knowledge of how to wean Lucy off a medication, I started with the one that had most recently been added and slowly, over seven days, reduced the dosage till it was stopped. I waited a week, and she was still seizure free. I began reducing the next medication gradually until it was down to zero, then waited another week. She still didn't have a seizure. Using the same procedure, I weaned Lucy off the third and final medication. It was miraculous. I went to get Lucy up one morning and she looked me right in the eye and smiled. I weep now as I recall that magnificent moment. At the age of four, I received my first genuine smile of recognition from my daughter, and my heart was set to burst with joy. I am filled with gratitude for Heather and her dedication and determination.

Every morning, from that day forward, I was greeted with eye contact and a beautiful smile. It felt like the greatest gift a mother could ever be given. Lucy remained seizure-free, without any medication, for several years. Eventually, I told the doctor what I had done, and he was surprised and a bit skeptical, but he accepted my decision.

I was ecstatic about this result, but Heather wanted more. She wanted to get Lucy walking. I had doubts that this would be possible but after our success in eliminating the seizures, I was willing to continue with the sessions every week. But Lucy seemed to lose interest. She no longer got excited on our way there and we could see no improvements in her efforts to walk. Heather changed; she became obsessed with the need for Lucy to walk. She advised me to discontinue using the ankle-foot orthoses (AFOs) as she believed they were interfering with Lucy's ability to learn to walk. I reluctantly agreed but the result was that Lucy's calf muscles began to shorten as her brain was continuously triggering the calf muscles to contract.

Heather didn't want me to see an orthopedic surgeon. She was convinced she could cure the leg problems with her healing energy, but the pediatrician was concerned Lucy's hips were seriously dislocating and I realized it was time to seek medical intervention, against Heather's advice. To me, a happy, alert child—albeit wheelchair-bound—was a huge gift. We discontinued the weekly sessions with Heather. In retrospect, I think I should have stopped things sooner. However, my desire to follow the natural healing route and to believe in someone who had already achieved a miracle, in my eyes, made me hesitate to stop these sessions for a few months after I instinctively knew that Heather could not help us anymore.

When we first encountered Professor Kerr Graham, the elderly Irishman who was head of Orthopedics at the Royal Children's Hospital in Melbourne, he scolded me for waiting so long and for discontinuing the AFOs. He said that Lucy's hips were too far gone for the radical new methods he was pioneering— Professor Graham had coopted Botox, the cosmetic surgeons' answer to wrinkled faces—for use in treating spastic cerebral palsy. But a few days after our appointment, I was surprised when he called and said there had been a last-minute cancellation, and we should come to the hospital tomorrow. He would do the surgery to release the inner thigh muscles to prevent further dislocation of the hips. He told me it was worth a try with no guarantee of success. The procedure involved cutting some of the muscle fibers of the adductor (inner thigh) muscles to weaken them and then injecting them with Botox to paralyze them for six months. Lucy was then placed in what's known as a "broomstick plaster cast" for four weeks. Her legs were stretched widely apart, placed in plaster casts from thigh to ankle and a "broomstick" was placed between them to keep her legs wide apart. The plan was to stretch the adductor muscles out to their optimal length, and once the cast was removed and they were still paralyzed with Botox, intensive physiotherapy would be used to build up the strength of the weak abductors on the outer thighs. This way, once the Botox wore off, the abductors could compete with the adductors and prevent them from shortening again.

A Huge Relief

The surgery was a success. It was a huge relief that it hadn't been too late. The lesson I learned was not to give my power away to anyone else, no matter how well-intended they were, and that I should have followed my gut instinct and stopped the sessions with Heather sooner. I also acknowledged that I should not abandon medical interventions altogether, as much as I had hoped to avoid them. I continued to pursue several other natural therapies, including homeopathy, but with limited success.

I also learned to monitor Lucy's response to everything I tried. She knew what was doing her good better than I did. She wasn't overthinking, she simply responded. I continued throughout her life to wrestle with every decision about what was best for her, often second-guessing myself and beating myself up if I felt I had made the wrong call. Other parents who had total faith that the medical profession knew what was best for their child and so didn't question treatments, could sleep better at night than I could. However, I have no regrets that I continued to question and explore other options. The prospect of living with a drugged-out zombie for the length of her life, like some of the other children I'd seen in similar circumstances, would have been soul-destroying.

Lucy did start having seizures again when she was seven years old and fortunately the mildest drug, Epilim, seemed to manage them successfully. She never returned to that drowsy, hazy state of mind that had muted her personality so terribly. Every morning, without fail, no matter how tired or depressed I felt, she would greet me with her beautiful smile.

This chapter would not be complete without touching on the topic of natural therapists and alternative healers who decide to cash in on desperate parents' hope for a miracle cure. The doctors and all of the specialists I met were mostly wonderful, caring souls, but they were unanimous in their condemnation of anything outside the mainstream medical model for special needs children. Our story unfolded 25 years ago in Australia, and I cannot say whether this attitude still prevails or if people have become more open-minded today. I do hope so.

One book I read that I found especially inspiring was *Awakened by Autism: Embracing Autism, Self and Hope for a New World*. It was written by Andrea Libutti, MD, a practicing emergency room doctor in the United States. When her son was diagnosed with autism, she followed all the suggested medical approaches and found none of them helpful. She began to explore alternative therapies and found a whole new world of possibilities which greatly improved her son's condition and changed her outlook on life, health, and medicine. That being said, there are, in my opinion, some unscrupulous people who offer false hope with expensive therapies. As open as I am to alternatives, the scientist in me persists. I am curious and need some background that makes sense to me before

I will lay out a lot of money for a miracle cure. I need to assess the motivation of the practitioner. Are they heart based, genuinely wanting to help? Are they motivated by fame and adulation? By monetary gain? Are they tapping into people's fears? When we are in fear and distress, we can be more easily manipulated.

During my travels around the world with my backpack, many times I needed to ask for assistance from strangers and I needed to quickly determine who to trust. This honed my skills in reading people. I have learned to trust first impressions and also to gauge whether I believe someone because I feel powerless and feel I need their help, or because I resonate in my heart with what they are doing and saying. Our heart is a powerful "truth barometer." Over the years, I have learned to recognize the feeling I get when I have encountered truth, even if my logical mind cannot explain why some new information could possibly be true. I get a felt sense like a huge surge of energy, emanating from my heart-center, and it floods through my whole body like a huge "Yes!"

Conversely, there have been times when I've convinced myself I needed to do something by thinking it through, but at the same time I have felt a heavy, contracted feeling in my heart, almost like a large rock has been placed on my chest. Every single time I have overridden this feeling and gone ahead anyway I have later realized that I was misled by my logical mind and that my heart had been right all along. I could have avoided making that misstep if I had trusted my heart. It is the same idea as "gut instinct," a similar contracted feeling that can be felt in the abdomen as well once we have learned to tune into our bodies.

Recently, I found this quote on a friend's Facebook page, author unknown, and it resonates with me:

"All we do comes either from Fear or Love. When we are in fear, we are in our head. When we are in our heart, we are connecting to love, to something bigger than just us."

About 12 years ago, I read Eckhart Tolle's bestselling book, *The Power of Now*. He explains what I intuitively felt back then. He defines this heart-centered response as tapping into our Consciousness or Beingness. It occurs when we are connected to the life force energy, our true nature, which is above the mind. He says that there is no need to understand it mentally, it must be felt, it's a "knowing."

It's my understanding that, generally, the feminine principle seems to be endowed with natural intuition. However, if social conditioning and upbringing leads to a lack of self-confidence and low self-esteem, we can begin to doubt this inborn gift and override it with conditioned beliefs, religious dogma, and cultural conditioning.

Several people told me I should take Lucy to Brazil to see John of God who supposedly performed miracle cures for many people with disabilities. Apart from the expense and the logistical nightmare it would have entailed, I didn't resonate with him. The idea of going gave me a contracted heart feeling rather than an expanded heart feeling. In 2020 he was arrested and is now in jail for multiple sex crimes.

Fear seems to cut us off from this natural inner guidance. If only I had been less fearful about what was best to do for Lucy, I could have made much better use of this skill during her life.

Chapter 7
Am I Doing the Right Thing?

Before Lucy came into my life, I had been a great sleeper and rarely did it take more than a few minutes for me to fall asleep after laying my head on a pillow. All that changed once I knew I was pregnant: my sleep was affected by the weight of the life-changing decisions I was making.

Not only did I worry about the impact on my unborn child of having no father present in her life, but I was acutely aware that my emotional state could impact her wellbeing. I worked hard at processing the emotional pain of being rejected by a man I loved, to clear it the best way I could in the quickest time possible.

After feeling her loving presence that solemn Christmas night before her birth I felt sure my baby wanted to be born, and I didn't trouble myself again about that decision afterward. But where should I live? A rental in Byron Bay was very expensive so I found a small granny flat in the backyard of a family home. It was basically one room with a kitchen in the corner plus a small bathroom. By moving the wardrobe between my bed and a sofa it felt like I now had two small rooms, a bedroom, and a living room. I had a two-door car. How would I access a baby car seat in the back seat? Now that I had no job I couldn't afford to upgrade. Fortunately, my generous mother offered to buy me a four-door car so that dilemma was sorted.

As soon as Lucy was born, my life was filled with weighty decisions and sleep seemed more mythical than ever. I suffered a lot of guilt because Lucy needed so much care that I was never able to take on full-time employment throughout her short life. I felt guilty that she needed a plethora of experts just to stay alive—the list included pediatricians, gastroenterologists, orthopedic surgeons, a neurologist, an ophthalmologist, a dietician, an occupational therapist, a speech pathologist, a physiotherapist...all of which were provided free of charge at the taxpayer's expense. It would have been a whole lot easier if I were the type of person who feels entitled, but I'm not. I keenly felt a weight of responsibility for the consequences of my decision to go ahead with the pregnancy. At times, when I reached my lowest ebb, I even framed the whole situation of having a severely disabled child as punishment for my selfishness.

I also realized how fortunate I was to live in a country that provided such extensive care and support for people in my situation. I heard horror stories about parents in the US who needed to pay out-of-pocket for every session with the physio or speech pathologist after their health insurance ran out or, worse still, they didn't have any health insurance to begin with. I counted my blessings many times over.

Although it didn't seem like I had a choice at the time, signing the form to authorize the life-support machine to be turned off when Lucy was only 36 hours old also weighed heavily upon me. Who can ever imagine they will be forced to sign their child's death warrant? Should I have resisted? Pleaded for more time? Or would that have been selfish on my part? Delaying the inevitable? The dilemma over bonding with my baby was excruciating. I desperately wanted to bond with my beloved daughter, yet part of me wanted to shield myself from the agony of losing her. I literally felt torn in two.

This continued for several months as doctors continued to prognosticate about how she would stop breathing one day. Or night. I wanted to be there when it happened.

I made the decision to literally sleep with Lucy in my arms every night. I wanted to know when she stopped breathing. I didn't have any plans to try to revive her, but I couldn't stand the thought that she would die alone, and I would find her in the morning.

The consequence of this decision was that my sleep became very light and every time I turned over, I had to move her to the other side into my other arm, which further disrupted my sleep. Lucy suffered from colic for almost five months and cried a lot. I walked up and down the short distance between the kitchen and the sofa, jiggling her, attempting to pacify her. So much for the advice in the book, *The Awakened Baby*, to let them cry out their frustration and not try to pacify them!

How did Lucy's father figure in all of this? I had only discovered that Hal was an addict (he was addicted to gambling—poker machines, to be precise) near the end of our relationship. He explained that he had moved to Byron Bay from Sydney to make a fresh start and had thrown himself into the Environment Centre and activist work to distract himself from gambling. I met him during his reformed stage. However, after he left me, it turned out that his new girlfriend was also a gambling addict and in a short time, he was visiting the poker machine venues in Byron Bay. I was quite disgusted by his fall from the pedestal on which I had foolishly placed him. Not only did I think of him as a coward but once he was gambling, I lost any pipedreams of him having a future relationship with Lucy. Once, before I fell pregnant, he had decided to visit his children in Sydney for the first time in over a year. He promised them he would take them to a theme park as a treat when he arrived. Since he was unemployed and didn't have the money for such a delight, I gave him enough to provide them with a great day out together. However, the night before the visit was to take place, he gambled the whole lot away so he couldn't take them anywhere. I was shocked when I learned this. I had no idea he gambled at that stage. And I felt outraged on his children's behalf. How could he do that to them? Once Lucy was born, the knowledge that he was an addict helped me to let go of my feelings for him more easily and focus only on a future with Lucy, just the two of us.

By the time Lucy died, although Hal was not addicted to drugs or alcohol, his excessive gambling had left him homeless living on the streets of Sydney in Kings Cross, the "Red Light" district that was a haven for drug addicts.

What I found interesting and even amusing was that after Lucy's death a social worker offered to arrange for the police to let her father know she had died. I told her that there was no way to locate him as the last I had heard, he had no fixed address and he was living on the streets. But just one hour later, the police did, indeed, track him down and notified him, at which time he called me. He sounded genuinely distressed and immediately said that he would drive to Daylesford and attend Lucy's funeral.

I perversely thought, "He's willing to come to her funeral—why hasn't he bothered to come and see her for the last five or six years?"

However, on the day of the funeral, Hal felt like a rock of support to help me hold it all together, especially at the funeral itself. I am very grateful to him for his support that day.

I Was Exhausted

By the time Lucy was five months old, I was exhausted. Mum suggested that Lucy and I fly up to Darwin where she lived so she could give me a break from full-time care. She generously paid our airfare and bought me a new big suitcase to fit all the baby accessories I needed to bring.

Then, a week before our flight, Mum broke her leg and had to be hospitalized. She arrived home just before we got there. Instead of the desperately needed break I had been anticipating, I suddenly had two people to care for. Mum couldn't use crutches. I had never heard of anything so ridiculous in my life! I had broken my foot once many years ago and knew how to use crutches. I tried teaching her how to do it. "It's easy," I said, "just put your weight on the crutches and swing your right leg forward to take the next step." She just couldn't master it. Every time she needed to use the toilet, I had to wheel her in a wheelchair to the bathroom (she couldn't manage to push herself along in the wheelchair either). Thankfully, she could maneuver herself out of the chair and onto the special toilet chair with handrails that was set up over the toilet. When she was finished, I needed to wheel her back down the hall to the living room. It was now up to me to cook all the meals, and wash the dishes and clothes, unassisted.

One day, friends invited Lucy and me to visit a nearby lake, a welcome short break from caring for Mum, who was busy chair-smoking in the living room. Darwin's tropical climate means that the windows are always open, but I detest being around cigarette smoke, so I looked forward to being outdoors by a lake. I spent an enjoyable afternoon cooling off in the tepid water and chatting with friends. Somehow, presumably from the lake water, Lucy contracted giardia parasites leading to extreme diarrhea and she had to be hospitalized. I found myself driving back and forth between the hospital and Mum's house, breastfeeding at the hospital, rushing home to wheel Mum to the bathroom and back, then rushing back to the hospital to comfort my six-month-old baby.

It was one of the nurses who saw my sorry state and called in a social worker. After I explained my situation to her, she counselled me that my daughter needed me more than my mother. Riddled with guilt that I was abandoning my mother in her time of need, I allowed the social worker to arrange for home help services to take over my mother's care so I could stay in the hospital full time. It was a huge relief to be able to focus solely on Lucy. The canny social worker also referred me to a music therapist working at the hospital. Those music therapy sessions were a godsend. Finally, someone was looking after my needs. I had no idea what music therapy was back then and discovered that it is a powerful form of psychotherapy. The therapist took me on guided meditations, continuously changing the recorded music as my journey progressed. I loved those sessions. After each one, we would talk and I could pour out my woes, especially about having to look after my mother, who had always seemed to play the victim role throughout her life. As the eldest child, I had always felt responsible for her, and I felt the need to rescue her.

One day, as I lamented my plight, the music therapist said, very matter-of-factly, "you sound just like your mother!" It felt like I had just been slapped in the face! I am so grateful that in her wisdom she gave me the biggest incentive to snap myself out of victimhood. I decided I was *not* going to be like my mother! I went back to the house and rummaged through a drawer containing the recordings of an entity called Lazaris, whose wisdom had been channeled by Jach Pursel. This had resulted in numerous books, lectures, and guided meditations that mother had collected over the years. I knew there was an insightful and powerful lecture somewhere about letting go of victim consciousness. I listened to it and found the accompanying guided meditation to be quite profound. The only bit I can recall 25 years later is the image of being stuck in thick gooey mud (victimhood), and then finding a way out of the mire. Before that I was still hampered by guilt at leaving Mum alone and wondering if I had done the right thing. This lecture and meditation gave me the clarity that, indeed, I had made the right decision.

I soon realized that I had made a mistake by saying to my mother that I would stay in Darwin as long as she needed me. Lucy recovered from the giardia, and we went back to Mum's house. After her cast was removed and she could walk again, she insisted she couldn't drive, despite the fact that the car was automatic and she had broken her left foot, which was not needed for driving. She wouldn't go shopping or visit her beloved local library. She was an avid reader and usually visited every week. She wouldn't take a shower for days at a time which is a problem when you sweat in the tropics. After almost five months of caring for Mum (who could still not give me any help with Lucy, our whole reason for the trip in the first place!) I was becoming impatient. I had managed to snap myself out of my victim role, thanks to the Lazaris tapes and the wonderful music therapist, but my mother was firmly and happily entrenched there.

I made a bold decision. On the day of one of my mother's doctors' appointments to follow up on the broken leg, I secretly booked my own appointment with the doctor several hours ahead of Mum's appointment. The doctor was a lovely woman and when I explained to her how Mum was still totally dependent on my care five months after the leg had broken, she was shocked. She had no idea how Mum had been behaving. "Leave this to me," were her parting words. Mum's friend drove her to the doctor, and I wondered what would transpire. She returned quite flustered and explained that this visit was like no other. The doctor had grilled her about how often she was showering, was she driving, had she been shopping? She had given Mum a list of tasks she had to perform before returning the following week. From what I gathered, the doctor had taken the tone of a strict schoolteacher scolding a recalcitrant student and had given a long list of homework that needed to be handed in on time.

My plot was never discovered, and the outcome was that Mum realized that she could actually drive the car and she could go to the library and do some shopping, get her hair done and take daily showers. Lucy and I were finally free to fly home. The trip had been a sober reminder that even if we feel like a victim, a change of perspective can completely change our lives. I slipped into victimhood several other times as Lucy got older, but I learned to catch myself more easily in the act and choose to do something differently; this changed my circumstances.

When Lucy was about four years old, I did start feeling overwhelmed by the responsibility of caring for her and Mum offered to move from Darwin to Daylesford. She bought a house in the small township of Hepburn Springs about five kilometers from my home and quickly made new friends. Her broken leg never healed properly as it hadn't been set correctly. The only solution was to re-break it, but Mum couldn't bring herself to go through that ordeal again, so she simply walked with a limp, very slowly, for the rest of her life. Although she wasn't a physical support, she was a great moral support from that point onward, accompanying me on the many trips to the hospital in Melbourne to see the various specialists involved in Lucy's care. Lucy cried a lot on those journeys and the heavy traffic frayed my nerves. Even parking at the hospital became an ordeal when hospital officials decided to enlarge the car park and temporarily closed part of it to complete the renovations. Traffic from both directions was fighting to get in through the toll gates, which would only open if there was an empty spot.

We had to wait for a car to leave before the next one could enter. One day we waited 45 minutes to get inside and while waiting, I saw some drivers get out of their cars and start a fist fight after one man said he was cut off by another. I was almost in tears when we finally arrived at the waiting room half an hour late. Having Mum there to soothe my frazzled nerves was a blessing.

Precocious Puberty

I was also shocked when Lucy was four years old when I noticed she began to sprout breasts and grow hair in her armpits and pubic area. The pediatrician explained that "precocious puberty," the diagnosis for this condition, indicated she had damage to the pituitary gland along with all the other brain damage she had experienced. The pituitary is the master time switch that triggers puberty, but it had malfunctioned and switched it on too early. The next thing the doctor said shocked me to the core. "We should think about starting her on the contraceptive pill." I reflexively answered, NO! What was he insinuating? He very matter-of-factly said that with all she had to contend with, pregnancy would be very hard on her. My mind was reeling. Who did he suppose was going to make her pregnant? I didn't dare ask.

Here began my biggest dilemma. My mind would not stop mulling this over and over. In his mild, calm way, the pediatrician was communicating to me that it was highly likely that Lucy would be raped. She could not speak, let alone fight off any perpetrator. The only possible place for such a travesty to occur would be in a respite home. She stayed in three different respite homes to give me regular breaks. One was a government-run home, one was managed by a not-for-profit organization and then there was Very Special Kids (VSK).

Health and safety regulations required all bedroom doors in these institutions to remain unlocked at all times. The respite homes took in children with a wide variety of disabilities and special needs. Cases like Lucy's were relatively rare; most of the children were intellectually disabled and very mobile. Autism, Down syndrome, and other conditions were common among the children in those homes. VSK had nursing staff on duty 24-hours per day, but in the other facilities staff slept overnight. What if a mobile child were to go into Lucy's room in the middle of the night? Most of the care staff were females but some were men. They could more easily handle the teenage boys who sometimes had angry outbursts. Was one of them a potential rapist?

The conclusion I reached was that the only way to ensure her safety 100% was to stop sending her to respite care. However, I had to admit that without these regular breaks, I could not cope physically, emotionally, or psychologically. I could burn out and then I would be unable to care for Lucy at all. I made the difficult decision to continue sending her to respite care, praying each time that she would be safe.

This decision came with a price. Each night, at about 3:00 a.m., Lucy would call out loudly, her way of communicating with me, to turn her on her other side. My sleep was so light that I would instantly awaken and go turn her over, arranging pillows to prevent her from rolling. She was soon fast asleep; however, my mind would start mulling over her safety. Would she be safe? How could she let me know if something bad ever happened? And the biggest one, what was going to happen to her when I was no longer able to care for her? This fear loomed over me, night after night, in the early hours of the morning. If not for me, who would be responsible for her? Who would care for and love her like I did? Who would have her best interests at heart? I could not stop my thoughts. I tossed and turned, with sleep eluding me.

Then, finally, about 30 minutes before it was time to get up, I would be exhausted, and sleep would overcome me. This pattern, unfortunately, continued even when Lucy was having a sleepover at the respite homes. I would dream that she was calling me to turn her and awaken with a start, only to recall that she wasn't there. Then the relentless mental imaginings would overtake my mind. Even after she passed away, I would still imagine I heard her calling me, always around 3:00 a.m., and I would startle awake. But by then I knew she was out of harm's way. No one could hurt her anymore.

I remember one day seeing people tossing coins into a wishing well and making secret wishes. I tossed in my coin and made a secret wish that Lucy would die before I could no longer care for her. I felt ashamed to admit that this was my wish. I never shared it with anyone. Even though this wish came from the deepest love for my daughter and the desire that she would always have a loving advocate, I suffered a lot of guilt about wishing for her death before mine. After she died, I met other parents with severely disabled children who shared with me that this, too, was their secret wish. What a huge relief to know I wasn't alone in this. It turns out that many parents of special needs children feel the same way. It is one of the wretched realities of life in that lane. Who will love them and advocate for them when we are no longer able to do so? Who will protect and encourage them? Our deaths condemn our children to lives of untold misery. It is an impossible situation, with no solace and no solution.

What if you, dear reader, were the parent of a child who will be totally dependent for the rest of his or her life? What would your wish be? What were the options for Lucy if I couldn't care for her? I was advised to have a document registered with the government to state my wishes, should I become incapacitated or die. I felt that I could not pass this heavy burden to either of my siblings and there was no one else I knew who could take over. I opted for a state-appointed trustee. But a trustee would not love Lucy, they would merely follow legal requirements for her care. She would be at the mercy of the staff in whatever institution she was placed. I do not blame myself for preferring her early death to this fate.

When Lucy was four, about two years after we had moved to the town of Daylesford, I started taking her to Riding for the Disabled (RDA). This program was run by a team of dedicated volunteers who were wonderful with Lucy. Being wheelchair-bound has many negative impacts on the body. However, it has been shown that sitting or lying on the horse's back when it moves creates motion in the joints similar to walking. Sitting on a horse also tilts the pelvis in the ideal position to encourage a straight spine. People who can only slump in a wheelchair can suddenly sit upright on a horse. This led to the invention of the Bambach saddle chair by an occupational therapist who worked at RDA. I bought one of these chairs for

Lucy that was specially modified with side supports to hold her in place. When she sat in her saddle chair, her back was amazingly straight. She loved sitting in it!

At RDA, the volunteers would place a sheepskin on the horse's back and lay Lucy on it. Her head rested on the horse's rump and as it walked, her shoulders would move a bit like arms do when we walk. The volunteers also sat her sideways and astride in the usual horse-riding position. Each position exercised different muscles and joints. One of the volunteers and I would walk along either side of the horse and hold onto her as another volunteer led the horse. Lucy seemed to have no fear, trusting that someone would always make sure she didn't fall off.

Lucy's Special Gifts

The only time I ever witnessed a child being mean to Lucy was at RDA. A child taunted her and was being hurtful and unfair. She did this to other children and seemed to delight in upsetting them. However, Lucy didn't react in any way. Some would say that she didn't know she was being teased, but I don't believe that. She always appeared to be taking in the world around her, although unable to participate much. My first reaction was to scold the child who was being mean. But then I watched as Lucy serenely looked at her and all the girl's anger and spite just drained out of her. There was no distress to feed off, so she simply stopped. This was another testament to Lucy's special gifts. She taught me that if we don't engage in someone's drama or negative projections, they can't sustain them.

Another little girl at RDA had a milder version of cerebral palsy. She could walk with a limp and could talk with difficulty and her grandparents were raising her. I can't recall what had happened to her father, but her mother had died unexpectedly in her early 30s. This older couple was kind enough, but the grandmother was filled with resentment that their retirement had been spoiled. Her life was now filled with taking her granddaughter to therapy sessions and she knew she would need to be responsible for this child for the rest of her life. I felt such pity for the girl who not only had lost her mother but now lived with someone exuding such resentment towards her. However, this was a better option than ending up in an institution, in my opinion. Through all her complaining, I could see that this grandmother did love her granddaughter and the grandfather seemed to be at peace with the situation and was very fond of the child.

Being a sole parent had an upside with regards to decision-making. I met other mothers who were keen to try natural therapies—which the doctors highly discouraged us from doing—but their husbands prevented it. Lucy responded very well to Reiki and other energy medicine techniques, as well as to music therapy. Yet in order for some of these mothers to try any of these modalities with their children, they had to either do it covertly or have huge discussions and arguments to bring their husbands around to their way of seeing things. What a blessing that I didn't need to convince anyone—other than myself—that it was a good idea to try some new approach! I also had the luxury of changing my mind without needing to justify it to anyone. My antenna became highly tuned to any subtle communication that Lucy might give me, and to my own intuition, which could communicate that something wasn't working and should be stopped.

Despite the many stresses, I loved being a mother. I was always making up little songs and singing them to

Lucy. The one she seemed to respond to the most started with, "Lucy is the best girl in the world, she's the very best girl in the world." I would sing to her as we cuddled on the sofa, or I bounced her on my knee. She was always well groomed and when she went for her two big hip surgeries, Professor Graham, the orthopedic surgeon, always made a point of complimenting me on Lucy's pretty hair styles with ribbons or scrunchies, as well as the colorful clothes she wore. I didn't like dressing her in hospital gowns. I loved taking her on outings to parks, to parades and shows and to visit friends. She joined me at classical music concerts, although sometimes I needed to feed her little pieces of chocolate, which melted in her mouth, to keep her quiet during the show.

She loved parties but sometimes got overexcited and very vocal, before becoming overwhelmed and starting to cry. For her fifth birthday party we invited some of the children from the childcare center. When she was excited, she would stretch out her body and sit up very straight and almost shout with joy, all the while making her hand signal for "Yes, I like this!" But after a while, I could see that she was becoming overwhelmed, and she started to cry. Nothing I did could stop her. Even after everyone left, she continued to cry for another 20 minutes. After this I was reluctant to organize another birthday party for her, but I am so glad I did throw a party for her ninth birthday, which turned out to be her last.

Lucy was also good at reading people. Many people wanted to hold her when she was little and she enjoyed cuddles, although with some people she would immediately cry, and I knew she didn't like their energy so I would quickly take her from them. But those with whom she did like to cuddle would frequently say afterwards that they felt so much better.

I believe Lucy was a healer. One day, Lucy and I went to Riding for Disabled to find one of the regular volunteers in distress. She explained that her 19-year-old son had just been killed in a motorcycle accident. She asked to hold Lucy, who was five at the time, and she wouldn't let Lucy go for over an hour. Lucy snuggled into her chest and when it was time for us to leave, the lady handed Lucy back and said that she now felt peaceful inside, so much better. When we reached home, Lucy started to cry. This cry was different from any I had ever heard from her before. It was filled with sorrow and deep grief. She was inconsolable. She cried for two hours straight, then stopped and returned to her normal self. I believe she had taken on some of the lady's unexpressed grief, and this was her way of releasing it.

Moving to Daylesford

I made the decision to relocate to Daylesford quite spontaneously. It was a small country town in Victoria, one-and-a-half hours' drive from Melbourne. I had previously only been there once to visit the famous mineral springs that are scattered throughout the area, and I knew of its reputation as the cold version of Byron Bay (it snowed in winter). It was a mecca for hippies, artists, musicians, and healers. Along with the communities of Ballarat and Bendigo it formed part of the Golden Triangle, which had been famous during the gold rush of the 1850s. Weekend prospectors still come with their metal detectors and occasionally find sizeable nuggets lying on the surface of the ground in dense bushland areas.

The fact of the matter was that living in Byron Bay was expensive. After our trip to Darwin with Mum, I had only been able to afford to rent a room in a share house with other single mothers. Lucy cried almost every night. I wasn't sure why and I couldn't seem to stop her. Sometimes she would start to cry at 5:00 p.m. and continue until the early hours of the morning. After a month or so, we would be asked to leave, and I would have to find another room in another share house.

My latest housemate, also a sole parent with a beautiful little three-year-old girl, said she wanted to have a talk with me one evening. Instantly, I knew what the talk would be about. She was going to ask us to leave. It was with a bolt of Divine inspiration that I suddenly thought, *I don't have to stay in Byron Bay*. The next thought was that I could move to Daylesford instead. I knew no one who lived there but the idea just felt right.

I didn't own much furniture or many household possessions, so it was not too difficult to pack up and leave. Some old school friends in Melbourne offered Lucy and me a room we could use while organizing rental accommodation in Daylesford and I felt so lucky to find a little two-bedroom miner's cottage complete with a large wood stove for cooking and heating. It even had a sunroom and a small garden.

What a shock to discover that renting the whole cottage was the same price as a single room in Byron Bay! Now Lucy's crying would not disturb anyone else. The next surprise was that once we moved in, Lucy hardly ever cried anymore. Was it the tranquil energy of the small town? Could it be the granite bedrock streaked with quartz seams containing veins of gold beneath our feet? On days when we had doctor's appointments in Melbourne, Lucy would cry on the journey there and back but as soon as we reached the outer limit of Daylesford, she would instantly stop crying. Daylesford suited her.

I began to realize that when I had a sudden burst of inspiration to make a particular decision, and followed this urge, unexpected and miraculous events could occur. There were long waiting lists for Early Intervention services in Byron Bay. However, on settling into our new cottage in Daylesford, as soon as we registered with the service provider in our region, the manager put Lucy straight into the program, skipping us to the top of the waiting list. We received free weekly physiotherapy, occupational therapy, speech therapy, and dietician services (including free formula and feeding tubes which I had had to pay for in Byron Bay).

Winter in the Central Highlands of Victoria is icy cold. The wooden boards on the floors of our miner's cottage were more than 100 years old and shrinkage had left gaps between them where the icy wind could blow in. Even after taping over the worst gaps with masking tape to stop the drafts, the heating bill was enormous. A friend suggested I buy a house instead of renting. *Impossible*, I thought. The next shock was to discover how cheap house prices were in Daylesford.

By cashing in my superannuation (supposed to be for retirements but available early in special cases such as ours), I could afford to buy a modest three-bedroom house with good insulation in the walls. After we moved in, I added insulation to the roof cavity as well. No more winter drafts—we were warm and cozy in our very own home.

This was a beautiful lesson for me. I had trusted a seemingly risky impulse to move 1600 kilometers away to an unknown place. It had been a 16-hour drive to get to our new home in Daylesford and, fortunately, we stopped with Lucy's father, Hal, in Sydney for one night, which marked about the halfway point in the journey.

Lucy was 18 months old at the time and her father hadn't seen her for many months.

My impulse to leave Byron Bay and relocate to Daylesford had a slew of unexpected benefits I could never have imagined. I have a strong sense that it was Lucy who gave me the impulse to leave Byron Bay, where the energy never suited her, and move to Daylesford, where she felt so much calmer.

Over time I realized that a pattern had emerged. Every time I needed something for Lucy, and had no visible way of acquiring it, I would worry and worry, trying to find a solution. As soon as I would give up, let go, and trust, something unforeseen would manifest to solve the problem.

When Lucy got her first wheelchair, it was too big for the trunk of the lovely car my mother had bought me. A car dealer somehow heard about my dilemma and offered to swap it for a slightly older but very reliable station wagon with plenty of space for the wheelchair.

When Lucy became too heavy to lift in and out of the car seat, I had no idea how I could upgrade to a wheelchair van. My friends launched a fundraiser for us and bought me an almost new van that had been set up for the Para-Olympians in the Sydney 2000 Olympics. It came with portable ramps and a track system to attach the wheelchair to the floor with straps. When the ramps became too difficult to use, a charity funded an electric wheelchair hoist to lift the chair effortlessly so I could wheel it in and out of the back of the van.

It became obvious that the worrying I did was actually preventing the solutions from manifesting sooner! Part of my resistance lay in thinking that I didn't deserve to receive help.

The guilt I carried around about being a burden on society and not pulling my weight (i.e., not earning an income), had made it difficult to open myself to receive help and—even harder—to ask for it. I have always been a giver, helping people in need. It came with some ego attachment that I was "in control," and that I was self-sufficient. The people I was helping were helpless victims, maybe I even thought of them as failures?

It was a big lesson in humility, to be in a situation where I needed to ask for help. At times I felt like I was begging for help, the ultimate humiliation in my eyes, but help always came in unexpected ways and I was so grateful to receive it. During this time, I had quite a bit of practice learning this lesson and I thank Lucy for putting me in the position to learn a valuable lesson in humility and for requiring that I open myself to receive help.

By age seven, Lucy had outgrown our cozy home. Her long legs hung over the end of the change table, and this made it difficult to maneuver it around a sharp corner in the hallway and into the bathroom. A ceiling track had been installed in the bathroom to lift her off the table and into the bath chair, but I could no longer get her out of the bathroom without bumping her feet against the doorjamb.

I couldn't afford to upgrade the facilities, which would have involved knocking down weight-bearing walls. Besides, I was lonely. Finding a partner could solve my problems. Looking back, I can see that at this point I began to feel helpless. This is not the state to be in when looking for a man, but I guess I had more lessons to learn.

Instead of trusting that my problems would be solved, I decided to force a solution.

Chapter 8
Marrying Dan

I had heard of a technique for manifesting what you want by putting out a very specific request to the Universe.

I decided to write a list of all the attributes I would like in a partner. First on the list: he must be a handyman. Secondly, he should not have full-time employment so he could help with Lucy.

My list had 17 attributes, going into great details such as: loves vegetarian food but is not a strict vegetarian. I had seen an article about old rail lines turned into cycling paths, so I added, "loves cycling adventures" to my list.

Literally weeks after creating my list, during a night when Lucy was at the government respite home, I attended an Open Mic Night at the local hotel. Dan had seen a picture of Lucy and me with our new electric wheelchair hoist covering the front page of the local paper. After I performed a belly dance for the large crowd, he strode over towards me and congratulated me on my performance. Tall and lanky in build, with sandy colored hair and a beard tinged with red, Dan cut a striking figure.

We talked for hours, and I told him about backpacking around the world. He also loved being out in nature, bush-walking and had been trekking in India and Nepal many years earlier.

One by one, Dan ticked every box on my list. He had retired early from teaching due to a nervous breakdown (here was a warning sign!) and he had fixed up an old cottage on a small farm—so he was a handyman! Born in the far North-West of Western Australia,

Dan had moved to Victoria as a young man and loved the Daylesford area. He invited Lucy and me to visit his small property, which he noted had several goats Lucy might like to pet – and he cooked me a delicious vegetarian meal. I'd asked Lucy before we went to let me know if she liked his energies. I trusted her judgment. When Dan asked if he could hold her, she snuggled in towards him and smiled. I took that as a yes.

Dan was soon offering to help us and was visiting us frequently. He wanted to start a relationship, but it all felt very fast. Before I knew it, he proposed marriage. I didn't want to remarry after being divorced in my late twenties prior to my world travels, but he insisted. He could see my problems caring for Lucy in our current house and suggested that if both of us sold our properties and pooled our resources we could buy a suitable place that he could renovate to be wheelchair friendly.

Feeling rushed to decide on marriage, I hesitated until my mother suddenly told me she wanted to leave the area and move back north to the tropics. This felt like a huge blow, as she had been my moral support through so many crises. But she became very distant after Dan appeared. I could tell she didn't like him, and he let me know that he didn't like her.

Although I felt some misgivings about his character, Dan was offering to be the "Knight in Shining Armor" who would solve all my problems. After all, he ticked all my boxes and even Lucy had given her blessing. But something didn't feel right. I was concerned about our age difference—he was 18 years my senior—and we had quite different tastes in music and movies.

Dan was also very judgmental of people he considered were doing the wrong thing, and he justified his behavior by explaining it was part of the culture in the local town when he had been growing up. One story he told me revolved around a car accident he had been involved in when he'd only been driving a short time. People had come running to the car and scolded him for being irresponsible. What? I'm sure most people I know would have run over to see if he were okay. But he believed this reaction was appropriate and correct. There were other subtle little things that I can't really recall now, but which bothered me. However, I overrode my misgivings to make the best life for Lucy. I accepted his marriage proposal, but I was in inner turmoil. Was I making the right decision?

We soon found an ideal home with a bathroom sharing a wall with a bedroom: it was perfect for cutting a hole through to connect the two rooms. With a ceiling track installed, I could slide Lucy in her bath sling straight into the bathroom. Dan and I both sold our properties easily and had enough money left over to fund extensive renovations. It felt a bit like being corralled into a trap, but I walked reluctantly yet willingly into it for the sake of my daughter's welfare, or that's how I justified it. On looking back, I can see that I had got to a point of feeling that I needed to be rescued.

Another red flag before we were married related to Dan's attitude to wandering dogs. Every time he saw a wandering dog, he would become enraged that the irresponsible owner had let the dog escape from their property. In his opinion, the owners should be punished. One day, he drove us along a country road and a dog started to cross the road. Even though I had been taught that we should not brake heavily or swerve to avoid hitting a dog, as it might cause an accident, in this type of situation my first reaction every time was to automatically move my foot to the brake, even if I didn't brake hard, to do my best to avoid hitting the dog. That day, I realized that not only did Dan not move his foot to the brake, but he actually accelerated towards the dog. My god, he was trying to hit it! Luckily, the dog was too fast and made it safely to the other side of the road. As Dan raged against irresponsible owners who should be punished, I silently contemplated what had just happened.

Dan had been married twice before. His only daughter from his first marriage had two daughters around Lucy's age. His grandchildren were her age! Wedding plans were steamrolled through, and I was to have three bridesmaids— Lucy and his two granddaughters. Lucy was ecstatic.

93

I recorded the message on her communication device that she was going to be a bridesmaid and when it was her turn to share her news at show and tell, she kept hitting the button over and over, until her aide had to take it away from her so others could share their news.

The wedding was fast approaching, and Mum had gone, not even inviting us to her farewell gathering, which mystified me. I learned later that Dan had told her to leave us alone, to pretty much "get lost."

Dan did a magnificent job of solving all the logistical problems of caring for Lucy. For this, I am greatly indebted to him. Not only did he spend countless hours on Lucy-related projects, but he also used his own money to fund most of the renovations. The new house was set up in such a way that Lucy would not outgrow the facilities.

Not only did he create a doorway between the bedroom and the bathroom so that I could effortlessly transfer Lucy from the hospital bed to the toilet or bath, but he also built a carport next to the house so even on rainy days the wheelchair could be loaded and unloaded from the van without anyone getting wet; he also installed a ramp for easy access into the house.

We no longer needed the garage in the backyard for a vehicle, so he converted half of it into a well fitted-out workshop for his many woodworking projects, and from the other half he created a beautiful dance studio for me. I now had time to teach belly dance classes, but more about that later.

Trapped into Marriage

On the surface everything looked great, but Dan had a brooding anger that only surfaced after the wedding. I never thought such an independent and capable person as myself would ever feel trapped into marriage, but I hadn't felt like I had had a choice.

Although Dan's mother had passed away many years earlier, he was still filled with hatred for her for being so controlling and turning him against his father after they had divorced in his early teens. It was a classic case of projecting his mother issues onto his wife. He never physically hit me, but the psychological abuse became intense. He wanted to control everything I thought and did, and he would fly into rages over trivial things. This was another huge lesson in humility. I had always looked harshly on women who stayed with abusive men, thinking of them as cowards, yet here I was staying in an abusive marriage, feeling powerless to leave.

I was willing to put up with the situation if it helped Lucy have a better life. Dan was very attentive to her, and she seemed to like him. Then things changed. Lucy had a difficult night and I had been up several times to help her, so I was exhausted. When it was time to get her up for school, Dan told me to sleep in, he would do it. He was feeling frustrated with Lucy for keeping me up all night, which had also disrupted his sleep.

I don't know exactly what happened next. One of the ways that cerebral palsy affects the body, for those with the spastic muscle variety such as Lucy, is that the strongest set of muscles are automatically triggered if any force is used against them. When Lucy was lying on her back, the only way to sit her up and not trigger the spasticity in her legs was to lift her torso very slowly. Otherwise, the hamstring muscles at the back of the thighs would be triggered and she would become as stiff as a board until the person backed off the pressure. When the pressure was gone, the muscles would relax, and her helper could very slowly bring her to a sitting position without triggering that automatic response. She had no control over it. She wasn't deliberately fighting her care-giver, although it could appear that way to someone unfamiliar with spastic muscles. Dan was fully aware of how this worked.

Lucy's leg muscles may have been overly strong, but her bones were not. Leg bones only develop strength through weight bearing and walking. Lucy spent time each day strapped into a standing frame to give her some opportunity to weight-bear on her feet but like most people who are wheelchair bound, she had osteoporosis in the leg bones. After the pins and plates were removed after extensive surgery to reconstruct Lucy's hips at age six—but before the holes in the bones had time to heal—I accidentally broke her femur (thigh bone) when I was changing her diaper. To place the diaper under her buttocks, I had lifted her legs and I heard a snap as one leg broke. I was mortified at what had happened and the consequences were that she needed to be placed in a half-body cast from waist to ankles for six weeks, further weakening her bones. After that, I was trained to roll her from side to side when replacing the diaper, rather than raising her legs and buttocks with my arm.

On this fateful morning, I can only imagine that Dan, feeling frustrated with Lucy who was nine by this time, fought against her spastic muscles and that was how he broke her leg. As he carried her out of the bedroom, in a fireman's hold over his shoulder, rather than hoisting her carefully into her wheelchair, I could hear her loud cries of pain, not her usual cries. Immediately, I jumped out of bed to see what was happening. After he placed her in the armchair where she could recline while having her tube feeds, I could see that one leg was not straight. I gently moved it and she cried out in pain, and it was obvious the bone was broken.

An ambulance was called to take Lucy and me to Melbourne to the Royal Children's Hospital. Although the ambulance driver drove slowly and with great care during the 100-kilometer trip, every time we went over a small bump she cried in pain. Already exhausted from almost no sleep the night before, my nerves felt at breaking point. Not for the first time, I wished so hard that I could take some of the pain she was experiencing from her.

I was already dreading the inevitable half body cast for six weeks where she would be bedridden once again. The challenge of keeping her cast clean around the "toileting area", where a diaper had to be slotted in between the cast and her skin to keep the cast dry, was a real challenge. My mind was filled with the logistical challenges ahead as we drove that slow and painful trip to the hospital. On arrival, she was X-rayed to determine where and what was broken. I was shocked by what happened next. I repeated Dan's explanation as he had told me. I fully believed, since I had accidentally broken her leg once, that this was also an accident. But the story didn't match with what the X-ray revealed, a very complex rotational fracture of the femur head. Dan arrived a few hours later and what appeared to be an interrogation began. Several different medical staff asked him over and over to retell the sequence of events leading to the broken leg. I was becoming upset. When I broke her leg none of this happened to me. Why were they picking on him? It was an accident. I was adamant.

It was only after Lucy died that our social worker—who we had known for years—confided in me that she had really wanted to report Dan for child abuse because the hospital staff had told her his version of events could never have resulted in such a break. But because I so adamantly believed it had been an accident, she didn't report him. This stunned me until I started looking at what had happened after that event with fresh eyes. Dan began pushing his body beyond its limits, going on grueling bike rides way beyond his fitness level, like a form of self-flagellation, punishment for his sins. But he also started to turn on Lucy, saying her dribbling made him sick and he banished her from the dinner table. He had frequent angry outbursts, flying into rages, and smashing plates and cups. When he found a book that a friend had loaned me about Meridian tapping (EFT) he saw that the publisher also sold tarot cards and he ripped the book up, claiming it was evil. It takes a huge force to rip the spine of a book.

He left home during the time Lucy was in the plaster cast, saying he couldn't take it anymore and he needed to get away. The cast needed to be on for more than six weeks. During that time, he came back, contrite, begging to be given another chance. I agreed on the condition he attend counseling for anger management. After his first appointment, he arrived home in a rage. Well, that didn't seem to have worked! I wanted to know who the therapist was and managed to get her number from him. I called her as he continued to rage and smash things and for the first time, a professional heard him in full flight. She told me to get my daughter and myself out of the house as fast as possible. I told her my daughter could not leave her bedroom due to the cast, we were trapped. Eventually he calmed down.

After that, the counselor began to give me sessions by phone, knowing I was housebound. She explained that Dan had presented as a meek and mild person, overwhelmed by the situation, tearful in her office, a victim. This is how he always showed himself. One time, I made an appointment to see his doctor and explain what was happening, asking him for help to get Dan some suitable treatment for his mental health, but the doctor was very dismissive. He said Dan was a kind and caring person and wouldn't believe what I told him. Dan was known around town as a bit of a hero for being willing to help such unfortunates as Lucy and me.

No Turning Back

Lucy was never quite the same after her leg healed, she seemed to lose some of her interest in life. I took her to a pantomime and while the other children were laughing and very excited, she slept through the whole thing. Dan was having another rage about something one evening and he directed it all at her. He yelled out, "She's a monster!" My beautiful little defenseless girl—a monster? This was the final straw. I knew there was no turning back. I needed to get him out of our lives permanently.

My only strategy for dealing with his rages was to stay completely calm until they blew over. I knew that his leaving had to be his idea, not mine. My instinct warned me that if I tried to throw him out, he could become very violent.

Dan had already rented a small cottage where he went to paint several times a week to get away from the stress of being around us (he found it relaxed him to create art). I encouraged him to move the spare bed into the cottage so he could sleep over when he became too stressed. Using patience and some reverse psychology, I helped him decide that it was best for him if he moved out permanently. This took careful strategy because in the past, when he realized that I was using psychology to "handle" his erratic behavior, he would become very angry and accuse me of using "stupid pop psychology" on him. He finally decided to leave Lucy and me for good about six months after the leg-breaking incident.

There was one significant time that I felt coerced by Dan to do something against my conscience. While I had been pregnant, I had attended a lecture by a woman who had unexpectedly stumbled on pharmaceutical fraud while helping to eradicate sudden infant death syndrome (SIDS). Her husband was an engineer and had invented a mat that could be placed under a baby and monitor its breathing. If the baby stopped breathing, a bell would ring to alert the parents. Pediatricians were excited and encouraged parents to buy one of these mats. However, a strange phenomenon occurred. Consistently, between 12 and 18 days after the babies were vaccinated (it didn't seem to matter which vaccine it was), the bells would ring to indicate the baby had stopped breathing. The child could then be revived. Was this a reaction to the vaccines? Pediatricians suddenly stopped recommending these mats, worried that parents would not continue with vaccinations. They began discrediting the mats and denied any link between vaccines and SIDS.

The couple was incredulous. Wasn't their mat saving lives? Were vaccines potentially causing SIDS? Doesn't this at least need to be investigated? The wife had a PhD in paleontology, so she was experienced at reading scientific reports. Now retired and with plenty of time on her hands, she obtained copies of any scientific studies she could find on the safety of vaccines. She not only wanted the final reports, but also all the raw data that had been measured and collated to come up with the final conclusions. Every study she found concluded that vaccines were safe and effective. But when she analyzed the raw data, a disturbing picture emerged. For example, the conclusions of an animal study might say that after five days, the animals were all healthy, indicating the vaccine was safe. However, the raw data showed that the next day, most of the animals died. This information never made it into the final report.

This researcher saw this repeatedly. Not one single pro-vaccine report that she found had actually proven the vaccine was safe. She began investigating to find out who funded these research studies and she discovered it was always the pharmaceutical company whose product was being evaluated— a clear conflict of interest. Next, she investigated SIDS rates worldwide and discovered that Japan had almost no cases. Their vaccination policy was to not vaccinate any child under two years of age. Could that be why babies were not dying of SIDS in Japan?

Next, she looked at the incidence of the diseases that the vaccines were supposed to prevent. Carefully studying the graphs, she discovered that the incidence of each disease was already dropping sharply before the vaccine rollout began so any improvements claimed after the rollouts were not statistically significant. However, graphs included in the final reports were making it look like the decrease was due to the introduction of the vaccines. This was done by changing the scale on the vertical axis of the graph. For example, in the pre-vaccinating graph they used a scale of 1-100 whereas the post vaccine graph would use a different scale such as 1-10. Yet, both graphs were put side-by-side as comparisons. Unless someone tried to check the finely printed scales and discover they were different, the graphs would lead one to believe that a vaccine had significantly reduced the prevalence of the disease.

I was shocked by this woman's presentation. During my time in the research lab in Melbourne, I had authored and co-authored several scientific papers, so I knew how it was supposed to be done. Here was someone with no vested interest in discrediting vaccines. All she was seeking was to understand why her husband's invention was suddenly being demonized for detecting that infants frequently stop breathing, at least sporadically over a short period of time, after receiving vaccines.

The couple went to the SIDS Foundation with all of these findings and asked if some of the fund-raising money from the "Red Nose" appeals each year could be directed to investigating a link between SIDS and vaccines. They were met with a resounding NO: none of the foundation's research money would be directed in that way. And, as it turned out, some of the biggest donors to the SIDS Foundation were pharmaceutical companies.

No Vaccines

As I left the lecture, I knew in my heart that I would not choose to vaccinate my child.

Eventually, along came Dan. When he learned that Lucy had not received any vaccines, he relentlessly plied me with pro-vaccine information. He claimed that all of the anti-vaccination arguments had been thoroughly debunked. Here was the evidence to prove his point, article after article on the Internet…even though I knew they were all based on the final papers with their manipulated findings. Lucy must be vaccinated. He became obsessed and would not stop until I had caved in. The one vaccine he homed in on was diphtheria/pertussis/tetanus (a.k.a. whooping cough)—the DTP vaccine.

Knowing in my heart that Lucy did not need the vaccine, I took her to the local doctor to receive the shot that Dan insisted she get. I consoled myself with the thought, that at eight years of age, at least Lucy was well past the danger age for SIDS. But how had I allowed myself to be so manipulated and bullied that I would go against what I knew to be right? I actually didn't believe Lucy would be harmed by just one shot, but it was the principle of the thing that rankled me.

I felt I had been forced to go against my conscience. How could I reconcile this? As I recall how I felt back then, I can see how dependent I felt at this time. I was not in my full power.

And what was Dan's motivation? Was he genuinely concerned about Lucy's welfare? Frightened for her health? I don't believe so. This was a power struggle. I needed to submit to his will. The effect on me was that I withdrew more deeply into myself. I could not be vulnerable with a man who felt the need to violate my conscience and subdue my will.

I had already learned about "projection," the idea that we project our unresolved issues out onto those around us. This understanding was very helpful in navigating Dan's difficult and often violent behaviors. I recognized that he was projecting his unresolved anger towards his mother onto me, which helped me to not take it so personally. His attacks on my belief systems had an interesting effect. It helped me to refine them. No matter what he said about Reiki energy, I knew in my heart it was real and I knew it was not evil. I could not be swayed. However, my belief in crop circles being created energetically, perhaps by extraterrestrials (rather than fakes created by tricksters, which is what he insisted was true) was open to scrutiny with any new incoming information I might find. But I did not "give in" to his will and change my belief in crop circles, just because of his bullying.

I had never heard of the term "gaslighting" until recent days. According to Psychology Today,

"Gaslighting is an insidious form of manipulation and psychological control. Victims of gaslighting are deliberately and systematically fed false information that leads them to question what they know to be true, often about themselves. They may end up doubting their memory, their perception, and even their sanity."[i]

102

I had the mental fortitude to not succumb to his attempted gaslighting. What happened instead was that I withdrew, I no longer shared my "controversial" thoughts and beliefs with him. One time when he was not around, I decided to look at his search history on the computer and found that he frequented sites like Snopes, a supposed fact checkers site. My research in more recent times has revealed that Snopes is funded by vested interests (corporations such as pharmaceutical companies) who purposely set out to debunk true scientific research that exposes their deceptions. Dan was being brainwashed by them! One dose of brainwashing in my youth was more than enough for me in this lifetime!

I'm not proud of myself for caving into Dan's pressure, especially as it meant going against what I believed to be in Lucy's best interests, but I have forgiven myself for my weakness. I now choose to forgive myself for all the compromises I made by marrying Dan. I recognize that I made decisions in a state of desperation. In hindsight, my mistake was seeing myself as a damsel in distress and thinking I needed to be rescued. There is a difference between being vulnerable and open to trusting that life will provide and being needy and fearful.

Yet, from a bird's eye view, my philosophy of life is that there is no right or wrong, good, or bad, only decisions and consequences. My decisions were not wrong or bad. This was an opportunity to "test my metal" and I learned that I still had a long way to go in standing up for myself and sticking with my convictions, regardless of the disapproval of others. I can now look at this time with Dan as a rite of passage. I needed to go through this to learn to set boundaries and realize that I could stand in my own power. I thank Lucy for helping me to reach a point where I finally stood up to Dan. It was when he started attacking her character that I realized he had stepped over that line, and I would take no more. After all of this was over, I have arrived at a place where I no longer feel the need to please others or justify my actions.

I have learned how resilient I am. I learned to what lengths I would go to do what I thought was best for my daughter, and that included marrying Dan. Back then, I overlooked some obvious signs that he was not mentally stable. One of the insights I got was that I had been very judgmental of women in abusive relationships. Now I knew from the inside why we make some of the decisions we do, especially when children are involved. How did I overlook the evidence and continue to believe that Dan had accidentally injured Lucy? I deeply regretted this blind-spot, after it was all over.

I have no regrets about my decision to straddle the worlds of mainstream medicine and natural/alternative therapies. This includes decisions to change doctors/therapists if I didn't feel one was on my wavelength.

In retrospect, I created a lot of stress for myself by delaying the termination of a relationship past the point when the doctor or alternative therapist no longer resonated with me. I agonized over each decision, prolonging my stress, before finally following my intuition. As soon as I did, doors unexpectedly opened with solutions I couldn't see before. An analogy that sums it up is the trapeze artist. As she swings to one side, there comes a point where she has to let go and fly through the air and trust that the "catcher" will be there to grab her on the other side. Life catches us when we dare to fly.

Lucy created many opportunities for me to practice having to let go and trust. Since her passing, I have come to trust my impulses even more. They may take me in unexpected directions, but they never let me down.

My decision to take full responsibility for Lucy's care without relying on Dan, knowing I would never take him back, set in motion an outcome I would never have imagined.

Suddenly, all my fears for her future vanished, literally overnight. As soon as she knew I would never take him back, Lucy left me the next day.

Chapter 9

Dealing with the Pain

I'm sure all parents want to do whatever they can to prevent or at least reduce any pain experienced by their child. Many times, I prayed that I could take on her pain so that Lucy would not have to suffer. But Lucy seemed to me to be fearless.

On the day she was scheduled for her major hip reconstruction surgery, my little six-year-old daughter lay quietly on the hospital bed as she was wheeled in to receive the anesthetic. I walked beside her feeling stressed and apprehensive. It was to be a long operation—six to eight hours—and her femur bones would be cut and set at an angle with pins. I was wondering if I were subjecting her to unnecessary suffering post-operatively.

But Lucy wasn't apprehensive in the least. As the orderly wheeled the bed around the corner, he miscalculated the turn and bumped the bed quite hard into the wall. She burst out laughing, much to our surprise. Lucy would cry out of pain and distress, but not fear. She was such a brave soul, and she was so trusting that life would take care of her.

After the hip reconstruction surgery it was natural that the pain management team was called in. I was shocked to learn that in the old days, the medical profession believed children didn't experience pain like adults, so often pain relief medications were not administered post-surgery. How did they ever come to that conclusion?

Nowadays, pain management is routinely used post-surgery because it was discovered if a child is pain free, they recover much more quickly. Fortunately, Lucy was born after the doctors learned their mistake. The initial operation to lengthen the tight and shortened adductor muscles and the Botox with physio had done a good job but the orthopedic surgeon showed me the X-rays of her hip joints. There was no ball and socket which meant that the hips would dislocate again in the future.

The femur bone in people who can walk has the ball on an angle, pointing in towards the hip socket. Lucy's femur was straight. The solution was to cut the head of the femur and use pins and plates to position it inwards, towards the hip socket. This was major surgery which lasted many hours and afterwards, Lucy had to be in traction for two weeks, lying flat on her back, unable to move. Pins were drilled into her skull and the sides of her knees so that she would be stretched out, which was distressing to see, I can assure you. The only good point was that there was no need for a cast as the metal pins and plates stabilized each thigh bone from the inside as it healed in its new position.

Complicating things was the fact Lucy had been experiencing gastric issues for more than a year prior to the surgery, vomiting after most meals. Several formula changes hadn't worked. The gastroenterologist advised using a pump to slowly administer formula so her stomach was never full, plus she was given medicine to help her stomach empty faster. Now the aides at school needed to be trained to use the pump and administer the stomach medicine. Even so, she was still vomiting at times.

To everyone's great surprise, all the gastric problems mysteriously evaporated after Lucy's hip surgery. Professor Graham surmised she must have been in a lot of pain due to the dislocated hips prior to the surgery—unbeknownst to us, as she had no way of telling me. Rather than make her cry, the pain instead caused her to tense up her abdomen and led to the reflux and vomiting problems. What a brave soul. She had been suffering in silence for more than a year prior to surgery. I am very grateful to Professor Graham for preventing years of pain by doing this important surgical procedure.

The post-surgery recovery was long and slow. Once Lucy no longer needed traction, the small scars in her head and knees healed, and the bones had been set in their new position, she needed extensive physiotherapy. The first time the physiotherapist turned Lucy on her stomach and flexed her knees, Lucy screamed in pain. I was in tears. The physio explained to me it was essential to stretch Lucy's quadriceps muscles so that eventually her feet could reach her buttocks. I had to grit my teeth and follow the daily physio routine at home, despite Lucy's cries of pain. Fortunately, after the first few weeks, it was no longer painful for her. She even enjoyed lying on her tummy. I sang her songs as we did the exercises.

We developed an after-bath evening routine where I would lay Lucy on the hospital bed, and before dressing her, we would run through her physio exercises. This had the double bonus of taking the pressure off buttocks she'd been sitting on all day in the wheelchair and allowing fresh air to meet skin that had been in a diaper all day. The hospital bed was donated to us by Daylesford hospital when staff replaced their old mechanical beds with electric beds. The bed fit into her bedroom and doubled as a change table and physiotherapy couch. This was a fantastic help to me. I could raise or lower it, and tilt it (necessary during the reflux stage), and the side rails prevented Lucy from rolling out. The bed could also be raised to a height where I didn't need to bend my back while doing Lucy's physio exercises.

Issues with Lip Biting

A disturbing habit that Lucy developed at about six years of age was to accidentally suck in her lower lip and bite it. The pain would trigger her jaw to spasm so she couldn't let go. The only way to stop the biting was to insert my finger into the side of her mouth and into the back of her jaw to unlock it. The result was that her lower lip was swollen and sometimes even bleeding for much of the time. Once, she accidentally put her finger into her mouth and bit it. Again, the pain caused her jaw to spasm, and I could not get it to relax and release the finger. She was crying, and I was crying, and feeling helpless. Finally, after repeated attempts over a period of ten minutes, I finally managed to pry her jaw open to find her finger bleeding from a wound inflicted by her teeth. Fortunately, she never put her finger in her mouth again, but the unintentional lip biting became worse and worse.

I consulted a dentist about the possibility of a mouthguard to push her lip out of harm's way, but he explained that would not work. I tried putting wads of cotton wool between the lip and the lower teeth but with all the dribbling, the wads didn't stay in place, plus there was a danger she might swallow one and choke.

One evening, I was at my wits end. Lucy's lip was a big, injured mess after a day of biting and crying in pain. I couldn't take it anymore so I drove her to the emergency room at the local hospital to see if someone could stop this. A kindly doctor was on duty and rather than looking worried about the issue, he saw this as a challenge, a puzzle that he would solve. After he spent a few minutes considering several possibilities, he came up with an idea:

What if we put cloth tape on the outside edge of Lucy's lower lip and stuck it to her chin to hold the lip out of harm's way? The adhesive on the tape was designed to resist moisture, so even when it was wet with saliva, it stayed stuck to her lip for a long time. He also suggested a small square piece of tape be placed on her chin. The tape sticking to the edge of her lip would then be stuck to the tape on her chin, rather than directly on the skin of her chin. This meant that each time the tape came unstuck from Lucy's lip and needed replacing, it didn't need to be ripped off the skin on her chin. His idea actually worked!

As long as the lip was dry when I first placed the tape along the edge, it stayed stuck for several hours before the saliva finally dissolved the adhesive, and the lip came free. Now, everywhere we went, I carried small squares of pre-cut tape, in order to be ready to replace the previous piece. The square on her chin only needed replacing every few days. What a huge relief to finally have a solution to save Lucy's lip! Yet, at the same time, I lamented the effect the white tape on Lucy's lip and chin had on her pretty face. I thought Lucy was a beautiful child, with her intelligent grey eyes, her rosy cheeks, her full lips, and her wide mouth. She hadn't inherited much of her looks from me but the one time I met with Hal's mother I could see quite a resemblance. Unfortunately, she needed the tape on her lip daily for the rest of her life.

Catheter Woes

A skill I wish I had never had to learn was how to insert a catheter. In the last year of Lucy's life, she began to have trouble emptying her bladder from time to time. Once the bladder became overly full, pressure could push urine back up towards the kidneys which the doctors told me was very dangerous. No amount of running a tap and hoping the sound would trigger the bladder to release, or pressing on the swollen bladder, could trigger it to empty. The last resort was to insert a catheter. This is quite an advanced nursing skill, and in some hospitals, it is only done by a doctor. It turned out that the entrance to Lucy's urethra (the tube connecting to the bladder) happened to be quite difficult to locate. One head nurse at the Ballarat Base Hospital poked around for more than 15 minutes, unable to insert the tube, with Lucy crying loudly the whole time. How could I ever stay calm when my daughter was in pain and crying and the head nurse was becoming increasingly frustrated? Yet medical staff expected me to do this myself at home.

I did manage to do it successfully a few times but usually I couldn't. My only solution was to take Lucy to the small Daylesford hospital emergency department, and they would, thankfully, do it for me. The staff there were surprised that I was expected to do this procedure on my own, and they were happy to help when required.

Lucy's stoma, the tube with a cap on it that allowed the formula to pass directly into her stomach, needed to be changed about once every six months. It was made of silicon rubber and the stomach acid would eventually cause it to deteriorate. Adults can cope with replacing the stoma without anesthetic, but children need to be anaesthetized. It's not a heavy anesthetic and the child comes around soon after the procedure is finished. One day, we had to queue for a very long time at the Royal Children's Hospital before it was Lucy's turn and someone new was on duty. When the orderly brought Lucy back, I could see right away that the stoma the new staff member had selected was not the correct size. It was infant sized, much too narrow for all my feeding tubes. The doctor who made the mistake apologized but said that it was not possible to anaesthetize Lucy again so soon after the anesthetic she had just received when the incorrect sized stoma had been inserted. The doctor would need to pull it out and force in the new one straight away. The inside of the stoma has a balloon that holds it snugly to the surface of the stomach lining.

It didn't take too much effort for the doctor to pull out the recently inserted stoma, but the lining of the stomach is designed to contract quickly to close itself when a stoma is removed. Since a smaller stoma had accidentally been placed there, the stomach lining had already shrunk to fit snugly around it. Now the doctor needed to squeeze a considerably larger stoma through that smaller hole. The doctor warned me it would be like being punched in the stomach. I had no idea of the force she'd use. It was horrifying to watch. Lucy screamed in shock, more than pain, and was inconsolable for the next half hour. I was tired, we had sat around in the clinic for hours waiting for our turn and then, we had to deal with this mistake with its violent consequences. As I tried to calm Lucy down, my sinuses were aching. By the time we drove the 90-minute journey home I was in a lot of pain.

Since infancy I have suffered with sinus issues and during Lucy's life, I did seem to contract more frequent sinus infections than at any other time in my life. They seemed to be triggered by stress. I had never had an infection take hold in such a short time or be so severe. By the next day, I was in agony. No natural therapies seemed to help so I went to my doctor, who took pity on me and suggested I spend a day or two in the local hospital for some rest. But what to do with Lucy? It was too short notice to arrange respite care, so the doctor admitted her, too, and we shared a two-bed ward. Instead of it being a time for me to rest and recover, however, at this small hospital the staff were inexperienced at treating such a high needs child as Lucy (she had always gone to either Ballarat Base Hospital or Royal Children's Hospital in Melbourne) so I had to teach them what to do to administer the feeds. It turned out to be easier to just do it myself. Eventually, I realized that this was no better than being at home, so we checked out early from the hospital.

I didn't handle Lucy's pain well. It created huge amounts of stress in me and impacted my health. It really helped when I took up hatha yoga while Lucy was at school. I loved those gentle classes and the teacher also invited me out to the nearby ashram to teach me the practice of neti, rinsing the sinuses with warm salty water using a special neti pot. The head was tilted on one side and the spout was inserted into one nostril, then the saline solution flowed through, to flush out the excess mucus.

I've come to realize much of my physical pain was a result of emotional stress. I wanted so much to do what was best for Lucy, no matter the personal cost to me. It was unbalanced and unsustainable. My nightly ritual, once Lucy was in bed and asleep, was to pour a hot bath, add some Epsom salts and lavender oil, and soak for a long time. This greatly helped me to get to sleep. One night, just as I lowered myself into the steaming hot water with a huge sigh of relief, Lucy started to cry. Oh no, what now? Anger and frustration welled up. All I wanted was some time to myself to relax and here she was, needing me again. A wave of self-pity overtook me, and I started yelling "stop torturing me, why are you torturing me?" over and over, bawling my eyes out in the bath. Then something remarkable happened. A part of me started observing myself ranting in the bath, believing this poor helpless child was torturing me on purpose. The absurdity of this notion hit me, and I burst out laughing at myself.

Of course, she wasn't trying to torture me. I heaved myself out of the bath, dried off and went to her room to sort out the problem. Then I topped up with more hot water and finished my bath. This reality check was profound. Her cries were her only method to communicate that something was wrong, never for any other reason.

A Creative Outlet

The best way I found to deal with the stress was to find a creative outlet. Once I discovered belly dancing and started performing in a duo with a friend who was also a single mum, I began to not just cope but to begin to enjoy life again. I now believe that the ability to express ourselves creatively is a key component to maintaining mental health when we are thrust into the demanding role of caring for a totally dependent child. For me, it was an essential key to retaining my sanity. Creative expression doesn't need to take the form of a performing art, however. It could revolve around gardening or cooking or craftwork, whatever makes our heart sing. And creativity isn't just important for carers. I believe we all need a creative outlet to stay fulfilled. Some people are lucky enough for their employment to allow them to express themselves creatively but for most of us, it's important to nurture our creativity in some other way.

A few years ago, I read the book by Elaine Aron called, *The Highly Sensitive Person*. She refers to these people as HSPs. What a revelation it was to understand t people's nervous systems are differently wired and some of us are highly sensitive while others absolutely are not! I appeared to fall into the *most* highly sensitive category. Rather than berate myself for this extreme sensitivity, I've now made peace with it and learned strategies to manage my nervous system so that I don't become overwhelmed as often as I used to. This knowledge would have been very useful during Lucy's lifetime. She was also highly sensitive and easily overwhelmed.

After discovering the term, I learned of a subset of HSPs called Empaths. After taking the quiz in Judith Orloff's book, *Empath's Survival Guide: Life Strategies for Sensitive People*, I discovered that I am also a "full-blown Empath." This means I can sense the distress of others, including their pain. I now believe that, yes, I was taking on some of Lucy's pain, but also that of others around me, particularly when we were in hospitals, which are filled with patients and their loved ones who are in distress. I now have an arsenal of tools I use to prevent myself from absorbing others' pain, anger, fear, and anxiety, but I also have techniques for clearing these absorbed energies if I do accidentally take them on.

Useful tools I regularly use are burning Palo Santo wood and smudging myself with smoke (moving the wood around my body). This instantly makes me feel more relaxed. I also wear black tourmaline or sugilite crystals as a bracelet or pendant. These crystals absorb negative energies so that I do not, and they seem to repel unwanted energies as well. I also routinely wear a BioGeometry pendant to strengthen my organs and promote good health. If I become stressed, I use Brain Gym® exercises to calm the nervous system or do heart-centered breathing exercise following HeartMath Institute method. But I've only acquired these skills and tools in recent years. I can see that Lucy was also an Empath and that's why she was able to heal people by cuddling or just being near them. If I'd been able to regularly clear her or use tools to prevent absorbing these energies in the first place, I wonder now if this could have reduced or perhaps eliminated some of her pain? We will never know.

Chapter 10

Making the Money Work and Getting the Support We Needed

Australia has a comprehensive social security system to support those in need. It is possible things have changed since I left 14 years ago, but during Lucy's lifetime, a lot of support was available.

I started out receiving a sole parent's pension which was barely adequate in the expensive locale of Byron Bay and probably most large cities around Australia but small country towns such as Daylesford offered cheaper accommodation which was a huge benefit.

Once Lucy was two years old my case manager suggested I apply for a carer's pension. The pension itself was the same as I had been receiving but we were entitled to many extra benefits due to Lucy's high needs. The government had closed all state-run institutions for children with disabilities under 16 years of age. It turns out to be a lot cheaper to pay parents to care for the children at home, and the children receive a better quality of life. But this puts a big burden on families and not everyone can cope.

My heart broke when I heard about families stressed beyond their abilities to cope who actually left their highly disabled children on the steps of Parliament House in Melbourne, abandoning them so that the government would be forced to look after them. These children were then placed with foster families. I knew I could never do this; I could never abandon Lucy, no matter what sacrifices I had to make.

Our basic living expenses were covered, helped by reduced phone and utility expenses for pensioners, rental assistance, and free healthcare services. However, if the car needed some expensive repairs or some other unexpected expenses arose, it was challenging to find the money. I have never bought expensive clothes or tried to keep up with the latest fashions, but now I found myself shopping for secondhand clothes in charity shops. I also began sewing many of our clothes. Being very tall and with extra-long arms and legs, I could now custom-make clothes that fit me. The spasticity in Lucy's arms made it very difficult to dress her; it was impossible to maneuver her arms into non-stretch clothing. Once I discovered how easy it was to sew stretch fabrics, though, I could effortlessly sew tops and bottoms that were easy to take on and off. Lucy dribbled so much that she sometimes soaked through four or more bibs per day. So, I invented super-absorbent bibs, buying the thickest terry toweling fabric I could find in colors that matched Lucy's school uniforms—royal blue for the local school, lavender for the specialist school. I cut a hole for her head and sewed matching ribbing around the neckline, making them easy to pull on and off.

I built a vegetable patch in the backyard of the house that I bought not long after arriving in Daylesford. I grew sweetcorn, tomatoes, capsicum, French beans, potatoes, pumpkins, eggplant, and many types of herbs. There were fruit trees already growing in the backyard—plums and apricots—and if I managed to pick them before the cockatoos found them, I had abundant stone fruit in the late summer. One year, when the plums were not quite ready to pick, I planned to wait another day or two for them to ripen. However, a flock of cockatoos landed on the tree and in a few hours, it was stripped of every single piece of fruit!

I grew strawberries bursting with flavor. I was in a constant battle with snails and slugs, even when I used all the natural deterrents that I had learned about through joining the local permaculture group. The most effective strategy was to collect the snails in a bucket and deliver them to my neighbor before they all slithered out; his ducks happily disposed of them.

In the winter I grew sprouts on sprouting trays and in jars—alfalfa, mung beans, lentils, and more. Gardening was very therapeutic. It got me outdoors and doing physical work in the sunshine and fresh air. I cooked nutritious and tasty pots of vegetable and lentil soups, adding some brown rice and millet to make them more filling. By making a full stock pot each time I cooked, I could then freeze portions, enough to last me a week or more. This allowed me to eat healthily and economically, even when I was tired or had too many other things to get through that day.

Before Lucy was born, I had always had a few massage clients on weekends and evenings to generate some extra pocket money, but once Lucy was born I decided to give up any ideas of continuing this. I was the one who needed to be massaged, and I was in no fit state to give to others. However, after Lucy started school, I did start massaging some clients from time to time. This really helped to fund any little extras and allowed me to save for unexpected expenses. This was the first time in my life I had needed to watch every penny I spent. In the past, I always had more than sufficient to meet my needs and fund any project I fancied. Now I felt I needed to justify every purchase. There were times when it became a choice between paying the electricity bill or buying food so I lived on whatever I could find in the pantry or fridge until the next fortnight's payment from the government arrived.

At least Lucy's formula was provided for free so I never needed to worry that she would go hungry.

Once Lucy started school, I had more time to earn money, but any regular work was out of the question. At any time, either of the schools Lucy attended might call me to say that Lucy had been rushed to hospital after a seizure or some other incident, so I was on call at all times. Any work I did needed to be flexible to cope with the sudden emergencies, so options were very limited.

Dan helped financial pressures greatly ease. Despite his faults, he was very generous, and this eased the heavy burden of managing expenses. He bought me an overlocking sewing machine, which made it a breeze to sew stretchy clothes. We ate more elaborate meals, and he took us on holidays and day trips. At least money stress had disappeared, even though other stresses took over.

Government assistance did not extend to personal vehicles, but did, however, provide half-price wheelchair taxi fares, helpful to those in cities where taxis with ramps or hoists are available, but Daylesford had no such luxuries. Private transportation was essential, especially considering the number of trips to hospitals in Melbourne (110 kilometers away) and Ballarat (50 kilometers away) and all the weekly sessions with physiotherapists, occupational therapists, and speech therapists in Ballarat. This was the downside of living in a small community.

I learned to receive, with deep gratitude, each of the vehicles that were donated to us. However, I realized that it was a lot easier for me to give than to receive. Overall, I learned that there are a lot of kindhearted and generous people in the world and the most important step was to ask for help and then be open to receive with love and gratitude.

Comprehensive Health Services

I honestly don't know how I would have coped in a country without such comprehensive health services. Maybe other countries still run institutions where children like Lucy are placed for life? Even with all the emotional and physical stress my life contained I would not have wanted to give her up to an institution.

Over the years, information has trickled out about the abuses inflicted on residents of institutions for the disabled, the elderly, and children under protective care. I would never want to willingly thrust Lucy into such a corrupted system.

One impediment to having full access to natural and alternative therapies was the cost. All the medically-based services were free. However, I needed to pay for anything outside the mainstream healthcare model. If money had been no object, I would have had more frequent chiropractic or osteopathic adjustments for my back. As it was, I waited till I was in considerable back pain before making an appointment, which is not the best way of receiving that kind of care.

Some practitioners offered me cheaper rates if they knew my circumstances but even reduced rates ate into my limited budget. I didn't attempt some promising alternative therapies because they were simply beyond my means. Heather, the lady who practiced energy healing on Lucy, was incredibly generous to offer all her sessions for free but most people needed to charge for their services as it was their full-time work. It is my opinion that the Australian Medical Association or AMA is controlled by pharmaceutical companies and most doctors oppose alternatives as their training does not extend that far.

After being immersed in the world of disability for 10 years I personally saw the positive effects of alternative therapies on other children, including those with autism, Down syndrome, and cerebral palsy. Maybe if some of these alternatives were supported by government assistance, more children could access them and ultimately save the government money by negating the need for some costly medical interventions.

Part of the Australian government's program to close institutional care facilities for all children under 16 years of age, and put the responsibility back on the parents, involved supporting the parents who were forced to become carers. Carers Victoria was a statewide nonprofit organization set up to support carers to cope with their role. This included those caring for the elderly or disabled adults, as well as children with disabilities. Once a year we would enjoy the official "Carers Week" and we were offered free massages and other treats. Carers Victoria also ran a lot of support groups for carers. It really helps to connect with others going through similar circumstances to your own. Only they can really understand what you're going through.

Lucy's high and complex needs meant that the support group that was the best for me was the Gastrostomy Support Group. It was designed to support anyone caring for someone with a feeding tube.

I'm so glad that I was able to successfully breastfeed Lucy for more than 12 months but sometime after that, things deteriorated. The sucking reflex that babies are born with goes away after two-to-four months, when an infant develops the muscle coordination to consciously suck. Fortunately, Lucy's sucking reflex persisted much longer. But with the motor part of her brain damaged, she couldn't coordinate the muscles required to suckle properly and she began accidentally detaching and biting my nipple during feeds. Ouch! I was unaware that with this inefficient sucking, she was no longer obtaining enough milk to sustain her and since she could only consume tiny amounts of puréed food, she slowly lost weight.

It was only when a healthcare worker noticed that she looked a bit thin that I took her to the pediatrician, and he realized she would need a gastrostomy button inserted so she could be tube fed for the rest of her life.

Lucy needed to gain weight before undergoing the operation so she was admitted to Lismore Base Hospital where they inserted a naso-gastric tube down her nose and straight into her stomach so that formula could go directly to the stomach. It was supposed to be a one-week stay, and once she gained weight, she would be transferred to Brisbane for the gastrostomy operation.

However, Lucy contracted Rota virus, a contagious form of gastroenteritis, that was rampant in the hospital at that time. This resulted in diarrhea and frequent vomiting from which it took her weeks to recover. Now she was even more underweight, and the staff needed to use a pump to slowly administer the formula, so her stomach was never full.

Sleeping on a camp bed in the children's playroom with the other mothers for six weeks left me tired and uncomfortable. Each day I needed to sit for hours with Lucy, frequently changing her diapers and her hospital gowns, which were covered with vomit. I chose to do these tasks myself, rather than waiting an hour for the overburdened nursing staff to have time to do it for us. And it was wearing me down. I needed a break to get away from the hospital.

121

Thankfully, my friend Jain offered to come in several times to visit Lucy and she always enjoyed his company. Now I could go out for some fresh air and sunshine, knowing she was in good hands. Each time I returned, I would find him telling her stories or drawing her pictures in his sketchbook.

One day, Jain asked if he could be Lucy's godfather. I was very touched and readily agreed. There was no formal ceremony, we just accepted that it was so.

It turned out that most of the children in the Gastrostomy Support Group not only needed tube feeding but they also had severe cerebral palsy and uncontrolled epilepsy. A small group of us would meet regularly to pour out our troubles, share our victories, recommend new doctors or alternative practitioners, and generally support each other in any way we could.

The social worker who organized each gathering would offer some counselling and provided us with refreshments. How I loved those gatherings! Here we were, a diverse group of women with virtually nothing else in common except our children. None of the group members had gone to university or travelled the world. They had grown up in small towns or on farms near Ballarat where we met, and yet we felt like family.

There was one time when I left home to attend appointments with Lucy in Ballarat and I completely forgot to pack the feeding tubes. I made a quick call to one of the mothers in the group and she gave me a spare set of tubes, so I didn't need to travel back home to retrieve my set. When each of our children was hospitalized (which happened quite regularly) we would visit the mother and child to give moral support and a listening ear.

Silent Communication

Four of the children were in the same class as Lucy at the special school she attended. The teacher would park their wheelchairs in a circle facing each other and inevitably, through what I can only imagine was silent (telepathic) communication, they would all burst out laughing at the same time. One of them must have just told a joke!

Carers Victoria produced a monthly magazine and they put out a call to carers to write about their experiences. They planned to publish a book with everyone's stories in it. The six best stories would be honored at the upcoming Carers Week celebrations. A gathering was planned at Parliament House in Melbourne and professional actors would read out the winning stories for the large crowd of carers and support staff in attendance. I decided that most of the stories would be on heavy topics, but I wanted to share an inspiring story about how I had overcome my depression by taking up belly dancing. I called it "Dancing the Blues Away."

My story was selected as one of the winners and we were invited to Parliament House; a well-known comedienne was chosen to read my story. Not only that, but they decided to finish the event with my story, after which I was asked to come out in my belly dance costume for a surprise performance. Here is a copy of my story:

Dancing the blues away

I take a bow and the crowd erupts with applause. I've just finished my first solo belly dancing floorshow at a local restaurant and can't wipe the smile from my face.

My mind wanders back two years. A friend calls. *"I've just started belly dancing classes. It's so much fun. You must come along and give it a try."*

I feel depressed, no energy, believing that caring full time for my daughter is all I have to look forward to. It's so long since I've done anything more energetic than lift my daughter or push her around the lake in her wheelchair. However, she's just started school, so I finally have some time to myself. *"Okay, I need some exercise."*

At first, the coordination is difficult, trying to follow the teacher who is moving her hips and her arms at the same time. Soon, it becomes easier but as soon as the teacher says, *"It's free time, move your body how it wants to the music"*, I freeze. What if I make a fool of myself? Why am I so self-conscious?

More than a year goes by, and I can dance three times as long before puffing. New moves come easily. I seem to have a natural talent, but *"free time"* is still torture. We are preparing for a Christmas performance in which each class is doing a group piece, but the teacher asks if anyone is willing to do a solo as well. Maybe this will push me through my inhibitions. I volunteer.

The teacher gives me extra time after each class. My routine comes together and with her encouragement, I feel myself expanding. I buy a sewing machine so I can make a costume.

My daughter becomes very ill and is hospitalized for two weeks. Feeling slightly guilty, I decide not to sleep over in the hospital each night as in the past during her numerous stays. She's older now, six, and the ward isn't too busy. The nurses know her well and will call me if there is a problem. I leave the Base Hospital each day at around 6pm and drive the 45 km home to sew and rehearse. Arriving back at the hospital by around 8:30 am, sometimes I bring in the costume to hand-sew the trimmings. During my lunch breaks I prowl the aisles at Spotlight looking for more fancy materials and trims.

The big night arrives. The belly dancers have hired out the whole restaurant. My daughter is discharged the previous day, so she comes along, my mum volunteering to sit with her while I'm dancing. Rather than nerves diminishing my performance, the presence of the crowd pushes me to new heights! The owner of the restaurant is surprised. He's only seen me in dowdy clothes pushing around the wheelchair.

"Would you be interested in doing a whole performance here on a Saturday night, say about 40 minutes' worth?"

I've just worn myself out doing a four-minute solo! It just pops out, *"Yes, but I'll need lots of time to prepare."* He's willing to wait until I feel ready.

It's time to get really fit. I sneak out of the house before my daughter wakes up in the morning and jog around the block. Surely, she'll be all right alone for 15 minutes. I do yoga stretches while she is having her tube feed for breakfast, stopping to mop up a vomit from time to time. I shift her therapy equipment out of the way in the lounge every chance I get and dance and dance. I'm careful not to swish the veil in her face as I fling it around or bump into her chair as I practice my spins.

The weight is falling off. I haven't been able to wear these jeans for a few years! As my muscles strengthen, lifting my daughter becomes easier. My lower back pain is now gone. During one of my monthly appointments, the chiropractor says, "Your back has improved dramatically!"

I'm still often tired after the broken sleep when my daughter needs to be turned or vomits in the middle of the night and I have to strip the bed but mostly I feel optimistic. There is more than just caring.

Five months later, I'm ready. The restaurant is packed, and I perform the dance of my life.

Elizabeth Huxtable

It was such an exciting afternoon. In order to enter Parliament House, we needed to go through a metal detector and have our bags searched. Imagine the surprise of the guard as he found my belly dance costume alongside Lucy's formula and feeding tubes in the bag. I explained what was about to happen and I guess he must have gossiped to others working at Parliament House. When I came out to dance, the walls of the auditorium were lined with Parliament House staff who came just to see me! I received a huge round of applause and then a line of people formed to congratulate me and thank me for my inspirational story. This became very overwhelming. It felt like I was watching someone else receiving all this praise and adulation. The story made it onto the front page of the local Daylesford newspaper, along with a photo of me in my costume.

Belly dancing not only helped me emerge from depression, but it also strengthened my core muscles, and this helped my back improve. Then my teacher retired due to ill health. As her star pupil, other students encouraged me to start teaching classes.

At first, I invited a few of the students to my home and we followed along to training videos in my living room. I found a new teacher in Ballarat and as my confidence and skill level grew, I began teaching beginner classes twice a week at a local dance studio located within walking distance of my home.

Dan would babysit Lucy to ensure I could always attend the classes. Now, not only was I keeping fit, but I was earning some money from belly dancing as well.

In addition to the dancing, after Lucy started school, I teamed up with a friend who was a playwright and actor as well as a single parent to create a performance piece for a women's mental health night. It included comedy routines, storytelling, and music.

Although I had never acted before I played the guitar and Donna and I sang and acted out the story together. Her script was about a mother with a disabled child who takes up belly dancing to overcome depression!

We finished the performance with me dancing a little bit. It was so well received that we were invited to create pieces for residents in nursing homes and other community events. They paid us a modest fee to cover our travelling expenses, but we mainly did these events for the fun of it. Donna had also struggled with depression but over a much longer period than me, and she had also overcome an addiction to alcohol. We were a great support to one another.

I believe that both the dancing and performing with Donna were essential to my mental health and helped me cope with the continual dramas of life as Lucy's mother. Also, my philosophy of life was that everything that happens is an opportunity to learn and grow. It helped engender resilience. I was determined not to be a long-term victim.

Handling Stress

I sometimes wonder why Dan couldn't handle the stress as well as me. After all, he entered our lives with eyes wide open, knowing Lucy's high needs ahead of time. On the other hand, I had had no forewarning of what was to come when I had walked into Lucy's world.

With no formal contact with the world of disability other than a distant cousin with motor neuron disease, I had quickly immersed myself in this new world of disability and embraced it.

Dan had had a nervous breakdown while teaching math at a high school and he had retired early. He was never able to resolve his hatred and anger towards his mother. His internalized rage–which he directed at himself as much as anyone else close to him–meant he didn't have resilience. If plans had to change at the last minute or some emergency happened, he would go into panic mode. He wasn't even responsible for Lucy's care! I made all the decisions and carried the burden of responsibility for her well-being, yet he was the one who panicked.

I had admired his lust for learning things. He had a very high IQ (something he bragged about), and regularly borrowed a stack of library books about physics, ecology, biology, and philosophy—always non-fiction. But I later discovered that he did this not for the joy of learning but because he desperately needed to know everything about how the world worked. He seemed to be frightened by the unknown, the mystical. He had a great fear of things that he couldn't explain. Things such as Reiki healing energy, inexplicable according to conventional science, frightened him so he categorized it as evil. All natural therapies were either evil or fakes. What a cynical way to view the world!

My more optimistic view of life meant that I didn't let the sudden emergencies affect me for too long. I would be propelled into action to sort out whatever was happening the best way I could. I was more spontaneous and impulsive, and I learned to trust my gut without needing scientific proof.

Marriages are particularly vulnerable to the stresses of parenting a child with special needs. The statistics in Australia back in the early 2000s were stark. The more severe the disabilities of the child, the more likely that child lived in a sole parent household. It was mostly the mother, but not always, who took on the full-time role after separation. I met one man who alternated with his ex-wife to be a full-time carer, six months on, six months off. This allowed him time to pursue a professional music career and he would travel extensively during his six months off.

Most of these children survive into adulthood and still need full-time care. After 16 years of age, they are eligible for group housing where five or six people with disabilities share a home where there are staff members present 24 hours a day. But these homes are not numerous enough to meet the demand. There are long waiting lists, and many parents continue to be carers for the rest of their lives. I heard about cases, particularly in rural areas, where a disabled adult only became known to the authorities after both parents died of old age. They had cared for the person their whole lives and never signed up for any government assistance.

I'm so glad I discovered the creative outlets of dancing and singing. They were essential for my mental health. Once again, Lucy put me in a position that forced me to expand and discover new things about myself.

Chapter 11

Calling on My Higher Levels and Learning to Love Myself

The family I grew up in was not religious although Mum was raised a Christian, riddled with guilt, until she decided to be an atheist in her early twenties. Even so, as children my sister and I attended Sunday school every week (my brother refused to go!) and we both sang in the junior choir at the local Methodist church.

At 17 I had many unanswered questions about the meaning of life, right and wrong, that my parents couldn't answer to my satisfaction. My first boyfriend was a musician who played bass in a band and when he invited me to one of their concerts, I willingly went along. However, I had no idea before we arrived that this was to be a performance by a gospel rock group that was supported by persuasive evangelists speaking about people giving their lives over to Jesus Christ. I was metaphorically "struck by lightning." These people seemed to answer all the questions I had been asking. They were welcoming and loving when I said I wanted to be "born again." Whereas my parents constantly argued, these Christian people seemed like the loving family I craved. Soon after joining this group of around 40 members, I was invited to play in the band—it was a dream come true! I was given a beautiful silver flute and told that I didn't need lessons, God would play through me. I had learned to play piano when I was young, however I had given it up at age 11. And I had played on a plastic recorder at school, so it didn't take long to work out how to play the keys. But I had no idea how to make the flute sound, so I did take some lessons.

Before each performance we "psyched ourselves up" with prayer, and energy rushed through me that we called the Holy Spirit. And, indeed, miraculously, I could play. I was given no music to play so I had to improvise. Soon, I was playing a Pan flute made of beautiful ebony wood and, eventually, an expensive gold lacquered saxophone. We performed evangelistic concerts designed to save people's souls around Melbourne, where I lived at the time. Soon we were touring further afield, to towns in the state of Victoria and eventually all around Australia. It was very exciting, but I felt a huge responsibility for saving everyone's souls so they wouldn't burn in Hell for eternity. The group, originally calling itself Alethia (Greek word for truth) was a breakaway from the Baptist church and our leader was a very charismatic man.

Then began what I later knew was brainwashing. I was told not to listen to my parents because the devil was speaking through them. I was taught all other branches of Christianity, including the Baptists, were wrong and, of course, all other religions were wrong. We had the exclusive, direct truth coming straight from God via certain members who received messages by "speaking in tongues" and others who were inspired to translate the messages into English. My logical, scientific brain was pushed out of the way ("logic is of the devil," they claimed), and all I needed to do was trust in these messages. At university I quit biology because the theory of evolution contradicted the creationist message of Earth being created in six days. Instead, I changed to chemistry. The Group didn't have any opinions about chemistry that contradicted my university lecturers.

Rejecting my family and former friends, I spent all my spare time with the group members. The band rehearsed once a week with amplifiers turned up high. To protect my hearing, I wore earplugs. There were weekly meetings every Sunday and all the unmarried members socialized together at other times, going to discos (this was the late 1970s) and hanging out together. Although I still lived at home while I was at university, my parents felt like they had lost me. As soon as I started work in a research laboratory, I moved out of my home into a granny flat in an elderly couple's backyard.

Once married to someone in the group, it was very difficult for one to leave and thankfully, after a brief relationship with the bass player, no one else in the group interested me romantically. Instead, I fell in love with David, who worked at the same research organization as me, and I am eternally grateful that he eventually helped me extricate myself from the group. After falling in love with him, I brought him along to one of our concerts, hoping to convert him, however, he was not interested at all. The group's leader and his wife paid me a personal visit and told me they received a message that Satan was over David's house and that I must never see him again.

I called off our relationship, but David kept calling me. Then the group leaders told me to leave the phone off the hook. Several days later, I was feeling bereft. The love of my life had been banished, and I felt heartbroken. Unexpectedly, my parents paid me a visit and told me that David had gone to see them because he was so worried about me. They wanted to know how I was, and what was going on. I poured out all my conflicted emotions and it felt like a huge relief. They were incredibly understanding and welcomed me back into the family. It felt like a healing balm. After our long chat, I decided to leave the group and resume my relationship with David. The leader of the group tried again to bring me back into the fold, even threatening that if I left the group, God would take away all my musical talents. But the spell had been broken, I no longer believed his words. I returned the musical instruments the group had provided, and I did not have anything more to do with them after that.

Five years after joining, I was finally free, but it took me 12 months to undo the cult brainwashing. I would start to follow a logical thought but then lose track of where I had started. Journaling eventually healed me. I would write down what I was trying to reason out in my mind and when I lost the thread, I could reread what I had written to remind myself. This was my most effective tool for undoing the brainwashing.

My biggest realization came just before I left the group when I realized: each religion and subgroup believe they have the ultimate truth and the others got it wrong. What if *all of them* have got it wrong? Once I left the group and religion behind, I went on a spiritual journey. I shunned groups and rituals of any kind, preferring to learn from reading books. Rather than believing all that I read, I followed ideas that resonated with me and left the rest. I recall reading one book a friend had recommended and only one paragraph resonated with me. But it had such a powerful effect on me that I felt compelled to leave a job I hated (teaching math at a high school) and take a new turn in my career. I took on four part time jobs I loved and that only took up around 20 hours per week, and still earned the same money as I had earned as a teacher.

Although I'd rejected organized religion, I still embraced the idea of a Divine Creator. The transcendent experiences of playing inspired music in the band were real, I just needed to re-contextualize them and reframe them from religious dogma to a new perspective. Two books were pivotal in my transformation. The first was *Out on a Limb* by Shirley MacLaine, in which the author shared her personal journey of discovering spiritual healing and channeling, and shared compelling evidence of reincarnation. The book didn't try to push an agenda, but rather just explored possibilities and alternative viewpoints. I fully opened my mind to infinite possibilities of how the world worked beyond the physical senses.

The second book that was key to my spiritual enlightenment at the time was *Seth Speaks*, a channeled book by Jane Roberts. *Seth Speaks* managed to pull the rug out from under all my previous understandings of reality. Sometimes, after reading just one page, I had to lie down with eyes closed to digest this mind-blowing information. All of it rang true, resonating through my whole being, even as I struggled to process it with my mind. Two profound concepts still stick in my mind. The first was the idea that multiple realities and dimensions all exist simultaneously. The author used the analogy of TV channels to drive her point home. All stations broadcast simultaneously but we can choose to switch to whatever channel we want. This helped me understand why so many religions claimed to be the only way to connect with the Divine. Tuning to a particular channel was their way to connect with the Divine.

Meanwhile, someone else was tuned to a different channel and that was their way to connect. Now I could reframe my question about religions. Instead of asking "what if they are all wrong?" I asked, "what if they are all right?" From their own perspectives, at least. This was so liberating!

No Fixed Truth

Leading on from that, the next bombshell from Seth was that we can choose our own truth because there is no fixed truth. He challenged the reader to decide to think a certain way for two weeks and evaluate whether that truth made us happier and more fulfilled. If not, try another truth for two weeks and see how that felt. This felt like the ultimate liberation. From then on, with each book I read I chose to be curious, and I would change my concept of reality using the ideas in the book. I would try on the ones that resonated for two weeks and decide what to keep and what to let go of, evolving my unique way of understanding life. To this day, I continue to evolve my view of the world, questioning any information I receive and evaluating it to see if it resonates with me.

I believe the guiding principles for understanding life, coupled with my powerful experiences in Egypt, raised my vibrational rate, and helped me navigate the ever-changing situations I faced during Lucy's short life. I was constantly open to new possibilities and alternative ways of managing her challenges.

One of the concepts my reading helped me to embrace, and which assisted me to cope with having a child with disabilities, was the idea that we have all chosen the circumstances of our birth and our life in order to learn and grow. The idea that this isn't the only chance we get to experience life helped keep me from feeling bad for Lucy and the fact she had such limited physical abilities. I didn't feel sorry for her in an overall sense although I naturally wanted to minimize her pain and suffering. But at some level, I believe she chose to experience life in a body that didn't work like others.

I met parents who spent years raging against their doctor and blaming him or her for their child's disability. One woman who brought her daughter to the Early Intervention group where Lucy received all of her physiotherapy and occupational therapy sessions prior to starting school would repeat, "If the doctor hadn't made mistakes during the delivery, our daughter wouldn't be in this terrible situation." Firstly, I felt sad that she and her husband were stuck in blaming mode, which made it impossible to move forward into acceptance. Secondly, I felt sad that their daughter was continually receiving the veiled message contained in her parents' anger that she was somehow broken and not what they wanted.

Elisabeth Kübler-Ross famously described the five stages of grief and noted that almost everyone experiences all five stages. First there is denial, followed by anger. Next comes bargaining, then depression, and finally acceptance. This is recognized as a linear process. What my experiences taught me is that parents of children with severe disabilities suffer from what is called "chronic grief." Because there is no ultimate endpoint of death, we may move through the various stages and reach acceptance, only to be catapulted back to an earlier stage by a change of circumstances. For instance, when our child starts school and we observe all the other children are being invited to birthday parties, but our child is excluded, it can trigger a fresh bout of grief. In retrospect, I can see that each time Lucy was hospitalized for one of her corrective surgeries, it triggered this experience of chronic grief in me. Just as I was hoping to extricate myself from the medical system, it seemed like we were thrust back into it. Once I became aware of chronic grief, it helped me move through the stages more quickly and back to a state of acceptance. If parents get stuck at one of these stages—such as the couple I observed still angrily blaming the doctor for their daughter's cerebral palsy— then it prevents them from moving on to acceptance.

My philosophy of life helped me acknowledge that on some level Lucy chose her circumstances and, also, I had chosen mine. I believe that something can be gained from every experience no matter how tragic or unfair it appears on the surface. Every challenge is ultimately a gift. It is up to us to find the gift. This perspective helped me move through each crisis, each plunge into victimhood and depression, and out the other side. It helped me make sense of a seemingly incomprehensible series of stresses. I certainly didn't move through them all elegantly, but my philosophy helped me bounce back each time. I now see that resilience is the most important attribute I developed, and it powerfully assists me to counter life's challenges. Whatever life philosophy we follow, if it leads to resilience during big challenges then it's working for us.

I fully comprehended that my priority needed to be my physical, emotional, and mental health when the pediatrician made it clear that Lucy could be sexually abused. As clear as it was that the only way to guarantee this could not happen would be to discontinue all respite care, the reality was that without any respite care my quality of life would be very poor. If I became ill—physically or mentally—then my greatest fear, which was about what would happen when I could not care for Lucy anymore, would have manifested itself.

Once I was settled with the decision to continue with regular respite care, I decided to closely monitor Lucy's behavior before going to each respite home. Although I couldn't seem to open that telepathic channel of communication that we had had during the pregnancy, I knew that Lucy would cry or get upset if she didn't want to do something. The first respite care she ever received was through an organization called Interchange. Unlike the respite homes that only took children five years and above, Interchange was open to babies and children of any age. Volunteers would host a child for one weekend per month in their homes. A childless couple offered to care for Lucy. They were thoroughly vetted, and the wife ran an organization that arranged care for high needs adults. She was already trained in how to give gastrostomy feeds and it didn't take long for her husband to learn everything Lucy needed as well—including administering medications like rectal Valium and how to handle seizures. Lucy seemed to love both of them and happily anticipated the visits to their home. When they split up, I was devastated. I assumed their visits would cease, but they both independently decided to continue hosting her. Miraculously, I now had two weekends off per month!

But there came a point when Lucy didn't seem to want to go to the man's house for the weekend anymore. At the same time a stranger approached us one day and apologetically informed me that Lucy was communicating with him telepathically and wanted him to pass on a message to me. He didn't know how I was going to respond to this news and was relieved when I was eager to hear what he had to say. He told me that although her physical body was like a baby's, she felt like a mature person and wanted to be communicated with as if she were an adult. She was five years old at the time! In my typical analytical way, after the initial shock of this news, I decided to try it out and see how she would respond. I began to chat with her less in a childlike way and more as if she were fully aware of what was going on around her and in the world. She seemed to appreciate my attempts to honor her intellect, even if I slipped back from time to time. I stopped playing her nursery rhymes and instead played her classical music on the radio. (I really can't stand pop music). Whenever she was stuck in half body casts while her broken legs mended, she would sometimes be on her own in the bedroom while I was attending to household chores. I would play the ABC Classic FM radio station all day for her. She didn't complain.

A More Mature Manner

When I explained to the wife that Lucy now wanted to be communicated with in a more mature manner, she was very open to the idea. However, when I talked with the husband about it, he couldn't bring himself to change. He thought of her as a precious little baby and doted on her, and he continued to relate to her in a baby-like way. He eagerly looked forward to her visits and I never thought for a moment that he would sexually abuse her—but Lucy didn't seem to want to stay with him anymore. I made a deal with her when her next visit was due. I told her that if she really didn't want to stay with him, she should cry when we got there, something she had never done in the past. As soon as we arrived, she started crying loudly and couldn't be pacified. When he tried to hold her, she cried harder. I was really looking forward to a weekend off. I had made some plans, but Lucy was telling me, loud and clear, she didn't want to stay. He was gutted when I told him I'd take her home. I felt a bit gutted myself! I knew he couldn't understand what was happening, I knew he felt hurt. He had been caring for her monthly for about three years by this point. He really loved her, but I couldn't ignore her communication. As difficult as it was for him and for me, I don't regret the decision to discontinue the monthly visits. She clearly did not want them anymore.

So, when I decided to continue using government respite care facilities, although I knew Lucy could never tell me if something specific had happened to her such as sexual abuse, I decided to trust that she would let me know if she did not want to go to a particular respite facility. As it turned out, the only time Lucy didn't want to stay in respite care was when my sister had her big fortieth birthday party. Lucy loved parties and would become so excited by them that she would eventually become overwhelmed and cry. Even though I didn't actually tell her I was headed to Melbourne for my sister's party, she instinctively knew she was about to miss out. She loved my sister. When I dropped her off at the respite home, she was usually quite cheerful meeting the carers and the other children. But that day, the quality of her cry was mournful and filled with disappointment. I could feel her willing me to take her along to the party. Feeling guilty, I left her behind. Logistically, it would have been almost impossible to take her to the venue, plus I wanted to be able to enjoy myself without having to check for feeding times, diaper changes and all the rest. I wanted and needed to attend the party without her. The staff reported that she cried for a long time after I drove away.

Fortunately, it was usually stress-free to leave her at the respite homes and these valuable times allowed me the opportunity to find the creative outlets of dance and musical performance. Belly dance turned into the most valuable pursuit on every level. First and foremost, I loved it. A sense of gracefulness and ease flowed through me as I danced. I was filled with joy and euphoria that I hadn't found through other pastimes. I had loved ballroom dancing passionately many years earlier, but the drawback had been that I needed to have someone to dance with. Belly dance is a solo activity. I could do it whenever I had the chance and the inclination.

Putting on a costume had an interesting effect on me. I was usually a conservative dresser, the responsible, reliable, dependable mother/scientist/teacher. Yet as soon as I was on stage in a costume, my alter ego came out to play: she was sensual, flowing, confident, and commanding of attention. People who knew me couldn't believe the transformation. Before taking up belly dance I was often hunched forward with my arms self-consciously covering my belly. After I started dancing my posture improved. My shoulders drew back, my chest opened, and my head rose regally from my neck making me taller. It was truly liberating for me, and I felt like I stepped into my full feminine power. I was vibrant, a goddess! Physically, my stamina increased, and my back improved through the building up of core muscles and better posture. Financially, I earned some money performing in restaurants and, eventually, teaching. I could never have believed how many benefits this hobby could bestow. Emotionally and mentally, it gave me something to look forward to, something pleasurable, just for me. I believe it is vital for anyone caring for a disabled child to find something, anything, that can take them completely outside the caring role. Time must be created to allow for this opportunity to fully express ourselves creatively. It's not a luxury. I believe it is a necessity. We may need ingenuity to create the space for ourselves. We may need to train someone to be able to safely and effectively take over our role—a friend or relative, perhaps—if we don't have access to formal respite care facilities. We also need to appreciate that we deserve this time off, that we don't need to burden ourselves unnecessarily with guilt over the false idea that we are abandoning our loved one. By finding our creative outlet, not only are we honoring and caring for ourselves, but we are enhancing our ability to care for our loved one.

When a carer plays the role of the martyr all the time it eventually breeds resentment and I have heard disturbing stories of carers who became abusive, taking out their frustration on the person they are responsible for. Don't let that happen! Be proactive. Carers deserve to have a life, too.

Chapter 12

After Lucy

By the time Lucy passed away, just two weeks before her tenth birthday, she weighed 35 kilograms and was very tall for her age. I'm almost 5' 11" (178 centimeters) and her father is well over six feet tall, so she inherited "tall" genes from both of us.

However, she only ever achieved the physical milestones of a four-month-old baby. She was unable to sit up without support, and she could not roll over; she could not use her hands, even to shoo away a fly crawling on her face. She could not speak, and she could only eat a small amount of puréed food, most of which ended up on her bib which needed to be changed several times a day due to excessive dribbling. Yet, she was loved by many, many people.

All of her classmates at the local primary school were attentive, patient, and kind to her. She brought out the nurturer in them, even the boys. They would hold her hand and guide the paintbrush for her during art class. They loved reading to her because she was always so attentive as they practiced their reading skills. And they told me that they could confide their deepest secrets to her because they knew she would never tell anyone.

When she first started at the local school, as I tried to maneuver the wheelchair into the classroom, children would rush past and allow the door to swing closed on us. But in a very short time they would see us coming and straightaway hold the door open to allow the wheelchair to enter the classroom. They included her in every way possible. Whenever I pushed her in the wheelchair up the main street of the town, children would run up to say hello to her. At her funeral all her classmates attended and made posters to celebrate her life as well as a book containing photos of all the activities in which she had participated while at school.

After the Make-a-Wish Foundation granted her wish to go to the theme parks on the Gold Coast, I put together a scrapbook of photos from the trip, as well as cut outs from brochures and magazines, so she could share her story at "Show and Tell". My heart almost burst with pride when I was invited to an assembly because she was to receive a special award from the principal for her book. Her aide wheeled her to the front of the packed hall to receive the award as the whole school cheered. I was so grateful for the way the local school embraced and accepted her.

After she died, I realized I had grown substantially as a result of Lucy's presence in my life, and yet I had grown dependent on the demands of caring for her. After the initial shock of losing Lucy so suddenly without warning, I needed to reassess my life. Two other girls from Lucy's class at the specialist school died around the same time, but they had spent many weeks in hospital, slowly fading away. Not Lucy, no painful deterioration. Once I learned what she came to teach me, off she went on her way, leaving me to pick up the pieces and start again. The coroner's report (necessary because she died while in the care of an institution) took a year to complete. They saved her brain for several months to conduct some studies on it and when the final report arrived in my hands, the cause of death was listed as, "Sudden, unexplained death."

Two days after she died, Dan came around and asked if we could get back together. I was emphatic. No, never. He made a big show in the local paper in the bereavement column, posting a drawing he had made of her, and saying how much he loved her and missed her. I didn't buy it. No doubt, he had regrets, but he had been resentful of her and the time I had spent caring for her, he had shunned her for the last six months of her life, and he had called her a monster.

I needed time to think. What was I to do now? How was I to earn a living? The government extends the carer's pension for three months after the death of the person being cared for so at least I had that time before I needed to earn money to survive.

Before Dan had left Lucy and me, he had said that he would relinquish his share of the house. However, now that she was gone and I wouldn't take him back, he wanted his share right away. I pleaded for time; I needed time to re-orient myself in the world. My life for the previous 10 years had revolved around Lucy and her needs and appointments, and handling the many dramas that comprised her life. Now I could make choices on where my life would go. But where did I want it to go? Could I go back to working in a lab? After all I had been through, all I had learned from Lucy, I realized how much it had changed me; I couldn't imagine going back to work in a lab again. However, I did look at what was available in Ballarat and there were almost no chemical laboratories there, none of them hiring new staff, and certainly nothing in research. I briefly considered teaching again, until I reminded myself of how stressed I had felt the whole time I had been working in a high school. I knew I would never fit into that system. But what was I to do? My mind was restlessly thinking of possibilities.

I needed time to grieve. Part of me was hugely relieved that Lucy was safe, no harm could come to her now, I no longer needed to torture myself about what would happen to her when I died or simply couldn't care for her anymore. However, the other part was deeply grieved at losing the most precious person in my life. No more morning smiles, no more cuddles. I was heartbroken to have lost her. She had been my world for 10 years. Almost every waking minute she had been in my thoughts. I was angry with Dan for not allowing me time to grieve and try to sort out what to do next. He went straight to a lawyer to force me out of the house. This meant that I needed to engage a lawyer to plead for more time.

Serendipitously, shortly after Lucy's passing, I bumped into one of my belly dancing acquaintances and after offering her condolences, she nervously asked me if I might be interested in a little group she was starting, a study group based on the book, *A Course in Miracles.* Knowing nothing about the book, but interested in her brief synopsis, I agreed to attend. When we had become acquainted at our dance classes, neither of us had had any idea of the other's spiritual beliefs, and we were both surprised to learn how similar our ideas and philosophies were.

This study group turned out to be pivotal in assisting me to regain my equilibrium. Not only was this lady a skilled facilitator—and she knew the material thoroughly—but it turned out that she was also a trained counsellor with many years' experience. She spent long hours outside of the classes counselling me, especially with regards to forgiving Dan and releasing my anger. During our married life, whenever Dan had gone into a rage, I had embraced a kind of stillness as I sensed it was the only way to pacify him. So, I was shocked to realize that now even thinking about him would trigger a panic attack. I had never felt such terror of a person in my life. What a shock to realize how much fear I had been suppressing! What I was feeling now seemed irrational. I didn't believe he would come into the house and beat me, but I couldn't stop my feelings of terror, so I changed the locks on each door of the house.

Living in a small town with a low crime rate for nine years, I had never once locked my doors, even if I spent a day away in Melbourne or Ballarat. Now I kept them locked all the time. I now realize that I was suffering from Post-Traumatic Stress Disorder.

This counsellor friend suggested applying for an intervention order to prevent Dan from legally coming anywhere near me. A social worker explained that without physical abuse—photos of bruising, for example—the case for emotional and psychological abuse was harder to prove. She explained that I would need to write quite a lengthy description of events and how I had felt during and after them. Instead of saying, "he did this to me," I should say, "when this happened," or "when he did this, I felt this way."

A Cathartic Document to Write

That turned out to be a difficult, yet cathartic, document to write! I spent hours writing it, reliving the fear, crying, sharing exactly how I had felt but had never been able to express during our two-year marriage. How powerful it was to write it all down. This exercise helped me to realize that I was not just grieving for the loss of Lucy, but I was grieving all the compromises I had made in marrying Dan, as well as my repressed anger at the way he had behaved towards both Lucy and me. The social worker said she had never read such a comprehensive application for an intervention order!

A court hearing was set. I could choose to be in a separate room at the courthouse, rather than in the court room with the judge and Dan. I was still experiencing panic attacks just thinking about him, to my utter surprise. If I was surprised at my delayed reaction, I'm sure Dan was mystified. He probably thought I was overreacting and being a drama queen, but I was not. These feelings of terror were real, no matter how irrational they were. I chose to wait in a separate room at the courthouse with the court-appointed social worker accompanying me. My heart beat far too fast, and my stomach was in knots. The court granted the intervention order for 12 months.

Dan's ultimate humiliation, I am surmising, was when he came to the house to collect his things. He now required a police escort, including the policeman who had released the doves at our wedding and whose daughter had been in Lucy's class at school. I had moved every item belonging to Dan into his shed in the backyard. I didn't want him in the house. Hearing his voice while talking to the police outside was triggering panic yet again. I was shaking all over. When would this end?

Meanwhile, I was trying to decide what to do with my life. Someone suggested that since I lived in a popular tourist town and my house was set up to accommodate someone with high support needs, I might consider opening as a specialized B&B? They proposed calling it Lucy's Lodge. I considered the possibility. The master bedroom was at the front of the house with an entrance and the main living room next to it. The other three bedrooms were in the back half of the house. There was a side entrance with a wheelchair ramp, a modified bathroom, ceiling hoists and a hospital bed. One bedroom could be set up for the parents with a queen-sized bed. There was a family room there, as well. All we would need to share was the kitchen, which was connected to the family room. This could work.

I applied to join the NEIS scheme (New Enterprise Incentive Scheme) a government initiative to prepare unemployed people to start their own businesses. My application was accepted, and I was given 12 months of financial support, equivalent to an unemployment benefit but without the need to search for a job. The training provided by the scheme included how to manage accounts, comply with taxation and accounting requirements, apply for zoning permits and market my business.

I enjoyed the weekly training sessions that were held in Castlemaine, a 50-kilometer drive from Daylesford. It was stimulating to meet the other budding entrepreneurs, sharing our excitement about the proposed new businesses we were starting. But one day, as I walked back to where my car was parked after the class, I noticed Dan's vehicle parked in the street near the library that he sometimes visited. Immediately, I was plunged back into panic and rushed back to my car, shaking with fear, hoping he didn't see me.

It was all well and good to be trained how to start my B&B business but how was I to secure the house? I couldn't afford to service the loan required to buy out Dan's portion of the property. A friend who organized lots of events, including the open mic night where I had first met Dan, offered to organize a huge fundraiser with a belly dance theme. She had many contacts and asked Bed and Breakfast (B&B) owners to donate their cottages to allow the top belly dancers from Melbourne to stay for

149

free if they would volunteer to perform. Other businesses donated goods and services for a giant raffle. The day arrived and the venue was almost full. There was so much goodwill to make Lucy's Lodge a reality. Dancers from all around the region came to watch the big-name dancers from Melbourne and we finished the night with a belly dance disco.

Exhausted, but high from the wonderful energy of the event, my heart fell as I counted the takings. How could this be? After covering expenses, we had collected around $5,000, a drop in the ocean of funds I needed to pay out Dan. All of the energy drained out of me as I realized that I still wouldn't be able to service the loan required. On top of that, there was much less interest in the accommodation than I had anticipated. Generally, families with high needs children and adults in wheelchairs expressed the desire to rent the whole house and not have me there while they visited. But where was I to stay during their visits?

One interesting tourist who did come to stay was a young man in his early twenties, a quadriplegic who needed 24-hour care. He had a team of three nurses who took eight-hour shifts. They wanted all four bedrooms but were happy for me to stay at the house. I set up a mattress in my dance studio for the two nights of their visit. They invited me to join them at the local pub and poured alcohol down the young man's feeding tube at his request, as we sipped from glasses of wine or beer.

Next day we all went on a tourist train to an historical gold mining town nearby. Wheelchair-bound since a car accident at the age of six, he was a journalist who focused on the issues of people with disabilities. He typed by using a probe attached to his head. There was a tracheotomy inserted into his throat which gave access for a tube to be put into his airways in order to suck out the mucus that accumulated there every 20 minutes, 24 hours a day. The accompanying nurses were constantly joking with him.

His visit left me feeling uplifted and I felt happy that Lucy's Lodge provided a way for him to get away from home and enjoy the countryside. One time, he told me, he even went skydiving, which had required a huge amount of planning. What an inspiration! But even with his promotion amongst the disability community, I still wasn't finding enough customers to make this work.

The lady who had been Lucy's Interchange host and who managed care homes for disabled adults told me about a 27-year-old woman with needs very similar to Lucy's, except that she could speak slowly and take food by mouth.

Her mother, after 27 years of caring for her had just thrown her out of her home after remarrying to someone who didn't want her around. Due to her high needs, it was challenging to find an appropriate share home for this young woman to move into. Would I take her in until they found her a place? Angela stayed with me for more than two months. During that time, I hoisted her onto the toilet when needed, spoon-fed her soft foods, and hoisted her into the bath each day. She also needed counselling to cope with being abandoned by her mother, so I became a listening ear.

My counselor friend from the *Course in Miracles* group also volunteered her services. We spent many hours around the dining table, encouraging her, and commiserating with her, as she shared all about her life with her mother and the shock of abandonment.

Working as a full-time carer, meant good pay, but one day, as I struggled to push Angela's wheelchair up the main street (this hill had never felt so steep when pushing young Lucy), I started to wonder what I was doing. A wave of despair flooded through me. This was what life with Lucy would have been like had she lived into adulthood. I started to understand why Angela's mother had had enough and didn't want to do it anymore. But Lucy hadn't lived, and I didn't need to do this anymore.

My lawyer was stalling Dan but selling the house became inevitable. When my brother, Tony, invited me to come and help him run his business in Malaysia, it felt like a lifeline had been thrown to me. Finally, it felt like there was some light at the end of the tunnel.

As soon as a suitable group home was found for Angela, I put the house on the market and sold off almost all my belongings. I kept only things that fostered creativity: some belly dance costumes and accessories, my flute and my guitar, and just two books from my large collection, including *A Course in Miracles*. That book had benefited me enormously throughout that first year after Lucy's passing.

The 12-month intervention order was about to expire. Dan still engendered huge amounts of irrational fear so the idea of not just leaving Daylesford, but Australia, sounded very appealing. I could make a fresh new start in a country where no one knew my past. Selling off all my possessions also became a cathartic experience. I was releasing, piece by piece, my old life, ready to embrace a brand-new chapter.

Chapter 13

A New Life in Malaysia

During my first 12 months in Malaysia, I did not have the luxury of falling in a heap and grieving deeply. I had one decision to make after another, and I always felt pressured around time.

Reconnecting with my brother, who had lived in various countries in Southeast Asia over the previous 20 years, was like a healing balm. He had recently escaped an abusive marriage and his vindictive estranged wife had been constantly sabotaging his business. We were amazed that we had been through surprisingly similar experiences, and we were both quite traumatized.

We had always been very close as children, but we had had no contact for many years after he had moved to Southeast Asia. It was such a relief to connect deeply with Tony again! We spent many hours talking through what we had both experienced in the intervening years. His business was selling wholesale golf equipment. Asian golfers love to upgrade their golf clubs to the newest and best to improve their performance.

Tony had just moved to Bangkok to tap into the huge Thai golf market and had left the small warehouse in Malaysia in the hands of his two staff members. There were some anomalies in the accounts, and this was why he wanted me, someone he could trust, to manage things. Little did I know that I was jumping from the proverbial frying pan into the fire.

I have no regrets about my decision to move to Malaysia but the first year was extremely difficult. There were several times when I seriously wanted to pack my suitcase and return to Australia but I'm glad I stayed.

Once I began to monitor the business and rectify the situation, both staff members decided to leave. I was left alone. The business was located in Ipoh, a two-hour drive from the capital of Malaysia, Kuala Lumpur. I knew no one there and my limited business training did not really apply to Malaysian regulations, plus, I knew nothing about golf clubs!

Tony sent his only staff member in Thailand to give me a hand for a couple of weeks soon after I found myself on my own. He and I were in constant phone contact. When someone called to place an order, I would call Tony to talk me through the steps to process it.

Not only did I not know the products that they were ordering, but I was having difficulty understanding the Malaysian accents over the phone. One time, I told the caller that I only spoke English, thinking he was speaking Malay, only to be told that he was, in fact, speaking English! By the same token, people were also having trouble understanding my Australian accent.

One day I was trying to give my telephone number to someone and every time I said the numeral "two," they would reply "three?" I would say "no, two," and they would reply, "three?" What was going on? Someone overheard me and told me to pronounce the word "two" the Malaysian way. Somehow, to the Malaysians, my Australian pronunciation of the "oo" sound did not compute. I have since learned how to say "two," Malaysian style.

How was I to find suitable staff? I had never employed anyone in my life. The one contact my brother gave me was an acquaintance with a wide circle of friends and she was a great networker. She immediately took me under her wing and introduced me to some influential people. One of them knew a woman who was an accounts clerk who had been out of the workforce while overcoming cancer and was now looking for a job. This man explained that this lady had years of experience maintaining the accounts for a business and she quickly accepted my job offer.

I had not thought to ask how long she had been out of the workforce. This was 2007 but her computer knowledge ended at the DOS era of the 1980s. She had never used a Windows-based computer or sent an email. Rather than admitting her lack of knowledge, she fudged her way through and played on my naïveté and gullibility.

My confidence was very low. I felt overwhelmed by the task of fitting into this new life with no one I knew there with me, and I felt ill-equipped to run the business. Every time I would ask a question about how business worked here, or how to write a letter to a government agency, my new staff member would speak down to me in a belittling way, as if I were quite stupid.

Fortunately, Tony was able to make a quick visit from Bangkok where he witnessed her bullying me and suggested I needed to tell her to stop. As soon as I realized the dynamic that was really going on and stood up to her, she immediately resigned.

Gradually, I improved at choosing employees, although not without a couple of spectacular failures. I finally ended up with a cohesive team that grew as the business began to flourish.

The business had been on the verge of bankruptcy when I arrived but when I invested all the proceeds from my share of the house in Daylesford into it, and got rid of uncooperative staff, and when Tony's ex-wife stopped sabotaging it, the business became successful.

Less than a year after arriving in Malaysia, on the second anniversary of Lucy's death—July 6th, 2008, I had an unexpected visitor. As I ate breakfast in my apartment in Ipoh, I suddenly felt a warm, loving presence behind me. It felt like someone was giving me a big, warm hug. I'm not one to remember birthdays and anniversaries but as I sensed that this loving energy was Lucy, I realized the significance of the date. Tears of joy filled my eyes as I bathed in her loving embrace. My heart felt like bursting open.

Exactly one year later, she stopped by again with another big, warm energy hug. Once again, I was not paying attention to the date until I sensed the beautiful, loving energy that surrounded me. And, so it continued, year after year.

Tony and I continued to support each other emotionally. He helped me navigate the business world in Malaysia and I helped him heal emotionally from his stormy marriage. I wanted to share the amazing concepts I had learned through the *Course in Miracles*; however, it was written in very complex language.

There were 365 daily lessons to follow, including homework, which was a big commitment. Being in the study group had kept me on track for a year, but my brother wasn't interested. Fortunately, a friend loaned me the book, *The Power of Now* by Eckhart Tolle and it echoed all the concepts in *A Course in Miracles* but in a digestible, bite-sized way. This book not only helped

Tony, but it also helped me understand the concepts in *A Course in Miracles* more deeply, and it helped heal some of my unresolved pain. I found Tolle's concept of the "pain body" fascinating and very relevant: it refers to old emotional pain caused by painful experiences in the past that have not dissipated because a person did not face them fully at the time they occurred.

A modality I learned in 2009, not long after arriving in Malaysia was EFT (Emotional Freedom Technique) and I felt immediate benefits from it. An instructor in Kuala Lumpur was running a weekend workshop to teach it, so I decided to travel down from Ipoh to attend. It still amazes me that such a simple technique can have such profound healing effects. It was a lifesaver when, a few years later, in 2012, my mother could no longer care for herself and needed to be moved to a nursing home in Australia.

I spent six weeks helping to sort out her things and make the transition. During that time, she triggered me repeatedly. I would excuse myself and as I walked outside, I would mutter under my breath all the frustration and anger I was feeling while tapping the acupuncture points that I had learned in the course.

EFT, also known as "Tapping," differs from simply reciting affirmations, in that it posits that before we attempt to reprogram our thoughts with a new positive affirmation or thought pattern, we need to first acknowledge how we are feeling right now. As long as we are tapping the appropriate points while we speak the words out loud, we are not reinforcing the negative thought, but releasing energy distortions in the meridians associated with the thought or emotion.

As I walked outside my mother's house I would start tapping and mutter, "she is driving me crazy. I can't stand her smoking inside. I feel so frustrated," venting all my pent-up feelings. The next phase is to affirm that maybe things could be seen in a different way. "Perhaps I can learn to see my mother differently?" Finally, we affirm how we want things to be, "I now choose to accept Mum as she is, instead of wishing she could be someone else."

After a lifetime of being triggered by her I finally found acceptance, thanks to all that tapping. When she passed away three months later, I felt a deep peace that she was finally able to leave her painful body and that I had resolved all my frustration and annoyance with her.

EFT and the Emotion Code

As soon as I completed the EFT course, I urged Tony to find a practitioner in Bangkok and book a session. The practitioner he found was very experienced and she also used another modality called Emotion Code. She was about to run a workshop to teach Emotion Code, which Tony found incredibly helpful, so he urged me to fly to Chiang Mai in northern Thailand and attend the training. Emotion Code is another energy psychology technique that is similar to EFT in some respects, but it uses muscle testing to find trapped emotions inside our bodies.

I stayed for a week after the training and had three private sessions where the trainer combined the two techniques, EFT and Emotion Code. This helped to facilitate some powerful releasing around Lucy's death. Many formerly unshed tears flowed during our sessions and after each one, I felt lighter and freer, released from the burdens I had been carrying around for so long.

Finally, I had found the practitioner and the modalities that could help me heal from the traumas. Fortunately, both techniques can be done online, and I had many sessions with my trainer over the next couple of years.

Massage in Asia is available everywhere at low cost, so I didn't bother to resurrect my massage skills, although I did start offering EFT/Emotion Code/Reiki sessions on evenings and weekends while managing Tony's business. But running an import/export company didn't fulfil me. The staff were competent and handling the day-to-day orders, so my task focused on troubleshooting and logistics. However, I didn't have enough to do in the office, and I became bored.

Back in 2010 while I had been visiting family and friends in Australia my mum had wanted me to take her to a psychic medium and she insisted I also book myself an appointment. After resisting and thinking I didn't need a psychic reading, she finally persuaded me.

During the session the psychic told me I was going to become a sound healer. What was that? I knew about music therapy (thanks to Lucy going to Darwin hospital all those years ago) but I did not know what sound healing was. The psychic knew a teacher and urged me to contact her. Synchronistically, this woman lived just around the corner from my father and stepmom. I booked myself a session just to see what it was, and I was instantly hooked.

The session made me feel more peaceful and relaxed than I had since way back before Lucy was born. I wanted to learn more. The teacher didn't have any courses scheduled during the short time I was there, but kindly offered to do one-to-one training with me the day before I flew back to Malaysia.

I learned how to use chakra chimes to balance energy centers, as well as gongs, tuning forks and singing bowls—both crystal and metal. This opened up a whole new world of possibilities.

My favorite sound tools back then were the chakra chimes, which were made in Byron Bay—and I later learned that the lady who makes them knew my friend Jain, Lucy's godfather. The therapist graciously sold me her set so I could take them with me the following day, saying that she would buy herself a new set. These are still one of the most helpful tools in my collection. I discovered that if I began my sessions by balancing a client's chakras with the chimes, then the remainder of the session using Reiki and energy psychology techniques became much more effective and easier to facilitate.

I was intimidated by the idea of using my voice as a sound tool but when I was back in Malaysia a friend forwarded me a link to a recording of Tom Kenyon's voice healing work. It touched my soul so deeply that I decided to travel to Seattle in the state of Washington to attend one of his retreats. Most of his sound work incorporates just one crystal bowl playing while he creates the most incredible sounds with his voice. It felt like these sounds could pierce deep inside me and clear any blockages from my energy field.

Kenyon had mentioned in one of his newsletters that someone was making a documentary about his life, and they were crowdfunding the project. I was so impressed with his impact on me that I wanted to support his work to reach more people; I donated to the filmmakers. I met up with them in Seattle and we instantly felt a lovely bond between us. A few months later, they requested help to complete the editing of the film in time to submit it to the Sundance Film Festival. After reading the email they had sent, the following morning, as I awoke, I felt a strong knowing that I needed to help them finish the film. By now I trusted these strong impulses. Mum had passed away and I had an unexpected inheritance, so I decided to donate some of it to the film and also to buy some expensive crystal singing bowls. The filmmakers thanked me profusely and because of this donation they told me I was now an Executive Producer of the film, and my name would go on the credits. This title simply acknowledges people who significantly finance a film, but it sounds very impressive! The film makers had followed Kenyon around the world for four years filming his work and interviewing him about his fascinating life.

After the event in Seattle, I flew south to visit the famous crystal bowl shop in Mount Shasta, known as the Crystal Room. Mount Shasta is located in Northern California, and it's where Eckhart Tolle had written his first book, *The Power of Now*. Mount Shasta is a dormant volcano that is part of a string of volcanoes stretching from Washington State down through Oregon and into California; it included Mount Rainier, which I had visited during my time in Seattle. This chain of mountains also includes Mount St. Helens, which famously erupted in 1980.

Mount Shasta is known as a major energy vortex on the planet, and I was intrigued about feeling the energy. The town itself is at the base of the volcano and it is a mecca for healers and artists—a bit like Daylesford. The crystal bowl shop had an apartment above it and keen customers like me could rent it cheaply if they wanted more time to test out various alchemy bowls to see what suited them best. These bowls are a patented design from a company called Crystal Tones which pioneered the process of adding other materials to the surface of quartz crystal. Crystal bowls are made by crushing quartz into a sand, then melting it and blowing it like glass. When the bowl is still hot, other crushed crystals such as amethyst, rose quartz, and even diamond, are coated on the outside and fused to the surface. Metals such as palladium, gold, and titanium can also coat the bowls. Each material adds its own quality to the quartz bowl and this process creates superb sound tools; they are very expensive.

I had planned to choose three bowls with the idea of creating a musical chord with them. I eventually left with seven bowls that could create three different musical chords. This was way beyond my initial budget. One staff member, Scott, spent hours with me selecting bowls that would fit together musically and which would stack inside each other to make travel easier. I was also looking for bowls fused with crystals that had the qualities to enhance my sound work, focusing on stress relief, clearing trauma, and creating deep relaxation and healing.

To complete the set, I needed a high G note, but we couldn't find a suitable bowl. A new shipment had arrived but was yet to be unpacked. Scott sensed that the bowl I needed was in the unpacked van. He suggested I come back in two hours when they would have finished the unpacking. Up until then, I had only focused on the crystal shop, so I decided to stroll along the main street and check out the many New Age shops established there. Only one attracted my eye: it had an Egyptian display in the window. On entering, I was immediately drawn to a display of CDs with Egyptian designs on the covers. I could feel a powerful energy emanating from them. My body began to shudder. The man behind the counter noticed my reaction and explained that his wife channeled the sounds and guided meditations on the CDs from Masters' and Angelic realms.

Activating the Chakras

The energy from the CDs was so powerful that when he told me there had been a cancellation and I could have a session with his wife right now if I wanted, I recognized that serendipity was again at work. It was perfect timing to fill the space before going back to the crystal shop. Sakkara Heartsong guided me through a meditation to activate my chakras and connect with my higher self. It was profound and by the end, I felt light and clear, and connected to my higher wisdom.

Recognizing that with Sakkara's help I could progress further in my life, we arranged two online follow-up sessions for when I returned to Malaysia. When I arrived back at the crystal shop, sure enough, the perfect bowl awaited me, and I completed my set.

The follow-up sessions with Sakkara greatly enhanced my connection to Source/Divine Creator, or whatever name we wish to give that Higher Power that guides us. I returned the following year to Mount Shasta, where I stayed for almost six weeks during a three-month trip to the United States.

During those six weeks I undertook a 17-day personal immersion/initiation with Sakkara into Egyptian Mystery School techniques, and I am now a qualified practitioner of these techniques. She took me to power spots on the mountain for some of these initiations and it was a profound opening to higher realms. During these daily sessions, we cleared more of my unresolved emotions such as grief and fear from this and previous lifetimes. This prepared me to move into the sound work I do today.

I had recently read a fascinating book about Kryon which mentioned Kryon's connection to the Pineal Tones Choir and synchronistically they were scheduled to hold an event in Mount Shasta while I was going to be there. The choir was designed to activate an energy node at Mount Shasta and was for participants only. If I wanted to attend, I would have to join the 400-voice choir. I hastily learned my part via recordings just before flying to the US and I found that singing the strange tones and words that made up the Pineal Tones was very energizing. During the final performance, the energy in the auditorium became so powerful that, at one point, I needed to hold onto the seat in front of me to keep my balance. I had sung in a 400-voice choir once in Melbourne many years earlier and it had been thrilling, but this experience at Mount Shasta eclipsed anything I had felt when singing in choirs previously. What a gift to be part of this incredible choir!

The main point of my journey to the US that year of 2014 was to attend the Globe Sound and Consciousness Institute in San Francisco to complete their Sound Healing Certificate Summer Intensive course. There was a six-week break between the two segments of the course, and during that time I went to Mount Shasta. The friendships I made with some of my fellow sound healing students continue till today.

It was a wonderful course, and it helped me realize that sound therapy was the perfect vocation for me. I felt so "at home" with the other students and the lecturers. Running the business with my brother had been a necessary steppingstone, but this was my path in life. One of my favorite parts during the training was when we took turns being the receiver of a sound healing session. All the other students, plus the teacher, together created personalized 20-minute sound sessions for each student.

The large room was set up with a gong, all sorts of drums and rattles, a didgeridoo, a crystal harp, Himalayan bowls, various crystal singing bowls, and other sound tools. In every case, those of us creating the sounds found a subtle connection between us, so that with no planning, a unique sound session was created for each receiver. We all intuitively knew what was needed and blended our sounds together. It felt magical. With 10 different lecturers—each with unique skills and areas of focus—the training was very comprehensive. We studied sacred geometry, music theory, the physics and mathematics of sound, the physiology of the body and how sound affects it, and the practicalities of setting up a sound therapy business. On an experiential level, we learned chanting and toning, and we attended gong baths, Tibetan bowl baths and TaKeTiNa sessions, which I found fascinating. Here is a definition from Wikipedia:[ii]

The TaKeTiNa Rhythm Process, developed by Austrian percussionist Reinhard Flatischler, is a musical, meditative group process for people who want to develop their awareness of rhythm.

This involved copying the facilitator who created increasingly complex rhythms by clapping, slapping the body and moving, until the logical mind could no longer cope with so many things happening simultaneously and we became transported into a kind of altered state of consciousness. I loved it!

My favorite lecturer was Sylvina Vergara, an Argentinian voice healer. She took us on guided meditations using sound, essential oils, and our voices to get in touch with deep emotional issues and traumas which we then released through our voices. This was the most profound sound work/emotional clearing for me personally during the course. I was able to get in touch with a trauma from my childhood and release it with my voice and movement, facilitated by Sylvina. I was so impressed with the effect this session had on me that I now teach her method to students in my voice healing courses today.

Attending the World Premiere

Not long before my proposed trip I had received some exciting news. The Tom Kenyon documentary, "Song of the New Earth," was having its world premiere at the Seattle International Film Festival, just prior to the start of the sound course I was taking in San Francisco. As an Executive Producer, I was invited to attend the premiere and at the After Party, I met the editor, animator, and film crew. The audience loved the film. I was very pleased to have played a part in bringing it to completion.

Following part two of the sound training, I joined the director of the movie and his wife at several screenings of the film, first at Ashland in Oregon, not far from Mount Shasta. I developed a lovely friendship with them, particularly the wife. She and I went on some adventures together, finding energy spots in Ashland and Mount Shasta. We then travelled to Arizona for the Illuminate Film Festival in Sedona, which specialized in spiritual and inspirational films, and the film was very positively received there.

Some filmgoers told us that they watched the film three times that week and each time they felt more healing from the magical sounds. Next, we travelled to Phoenix, AZ, where the film met with an appreciative crowd once again. I got to hear all of the Q&A sessions that were held after each screening and learned more about the behind-the-scenes details of making the film.

The following year, the director and his wife asked me if I would tour with the film in Australia and New Zealand. After having listened to so many of the Q&A sessions, I was able to offer my own Q&A sessions after each screening, starting in Queensland and working my way down the East Coast of Australia to Melbourne, then flying to Auckland, New Zealand.

To date, I have probably seen the film more than 50 times and I still love the effects Tom Kenyon's sound segments, scattered throughout the film, have on me.

After qualifying as a certified sound therapist, I returned to Malaysia and set up a company, Scientific Sound Asia, to start my new career in sound therapy. I loved the lifestyle in the quiet city of Ipoh, but it was not possible to find enough opportunities in a conservative community where people didn't know what sound therapy was and were not interested enough to find out. It was time to relocate to Kuala Lumpur, the capital of Malaysia. After more than eight years in Ipoh, and with many friends there, I felt conflicted about leaving. Kuala Lumpur is a large, busy, stressful city and I much prefer a quiet life closer to Nature, but I have managed to find my place here.

I still miss Lucy, and I sometimes marvel at the huge changes I have been through, and which have brought me to where I am today. The patience, flexibility, and acceptance—as well as the unconditional love—Lucy taught me are integral parts of the work I do and the way I manage my life.

One year, Lucy's godfather, Jain, was invited to present at Ubiquity University's annual Wisdom School event in Chartres, France, held annually during the first week of July. Jain was shy about presenting there for the first time and encouraged me to come along to give him some moral support.

By this point, I had left Tony's business and was working full time as a sound therapist. It took a leap of faith two years earlier, to leave the security of what had become a very successful business with my brother and strike out on my own, but I felt compelled to do it. It seemed like the perfect confluence of my love of playing music with my interest in healing.

Healing had always been my hobby but after taking the sound training in San Francisco and becoming a fully certified sound therapist, it developed into a passion. Tony offered the opportunity to return to the business after my three months in the United States, but I knew deep down it was time to start a new chapter and pursue sound therapy full time. By the time Jain invited me to the Wisdom School event, I had already scheduled some sound events in Germany and Switzerland, thanks to a healer I knew from Malaysia. She was a Qi Gong instructor and we had successfully collaborated with events in Malaysia, so when she invited me to join her in Europe, I eagerly took up her offer. After Jain's invitation, I rearranged my schedule to include the trip to Chartres as well. What clinched the decision to attend the Wisdom School event was finding out that the program included private access for our group to walk the famous labyrinth in Chartres Cathedral.

I had walked a labyrinth for the first time in Singapore on an Eckhart Tolle-style silent retreat. The venue had a reproduction of the intricate design of the

Chartres labyrinth painted onto an expanse of concrete the size of a basketball court. Walking the labyrinth slowly and mindfully was a profound experience for me. After reaching the center, energy surged through my body and I almost felt like dancing my way back out of the labyrinth, I was in such a state of ecstatic bliss.

The Chartres Labyrinth

The idea of walking the original labyrinth inside Chartres Cathedral, a famous energy site, was thrilling. Our group assembled outside the cathedral to await entry and I felt stomach cramps and an intense pressure on my chest. I needed to sit down on the cathedral steps, and I wondered if I might need to miss out on this highly anticipated event. Fortunately, when we were allowed inside, half of us were asked to wait while the first half of the group queued up to enter the labyrinth, one at a time. I took the opportunity to sit by myself, taking stock of how I was feeling and soaking up the sublime energies of the cathedral. I hoped I would feel well enough to walk the labyrinth after the first group were finished.

Suddenly, I felt Lucy's warm presence behind me, comforting me and she communicated somehow, that she wanted to walk the labyrinth with me. Yes, what a wonderful idea! The pressure on my chest was gone. My stomach no longer cramped. She must have needed me to sit alone, to give her time to connect with me before I queued up for my turn.

As I walked, I felt her loving presence on my shoulders, like I was carrying her around the twists and turns of this symbolic life journey to the center of the labyrinth and back out. It was the evening of July 5 and after a quick calculation, I realized it was 6:00 a.m. in

Australia, the time I had learned of Lucy's death, exactly 12 years earlier. Tears of gratitude flowed freely for all she had taught me, and how much I had grown since she had passed over.

The final night of the Wisdom School event included an open stage performance night, and all participants were encouraged to offer a short performance, a song, a poem or whatever we wished to share. After the labyrinth walk, Lucy told me that she wanted to play through my flute at the performance night. I didn't want to do it. This beautiful connection with her on the labyrinth felt so precious and special and private, but she was adamant. At the last minute, after the program had already been arranged, I relented and asked the organizer to squeeze me into the program, promising not to take too long. I had no idea what Lucy wanted to play but I trusted the sounds would come to me at the right time.

Feeling a bit nervous, when my turn came, I walked to the front of the audience, flute in hand, and shared with everyone my experience of walking the labyrinth with Lucy. Then I told them that she wanted to play the flute through me. I always close my eyes when I play the flute and as I played a sweet but sad melody, I could feel her expressing grief and sadness through the music, helping someone in the audience who had been unable to express it, just like all those years ago when the RDA volunteer had lost her son.

As the sweet sounds of the flute played, I could hear people sobbing throughout the auditorium. The improvisation was in three-quarter time (waltz time), and I had never improvised to that signature before. Since that day, I sometimes feel Lucy's presence during a sound bath, urging me to play my flute.

As I play, it is always waltz time and sorrowful and I can sense that someone in the audience is holding onto unexpressed grief that Lucy is helping to express for them. I think she is helping me to express my grief, too.

As I stepped into the elevator on my way back to my room that day, one of the Wisdom School participants stepped in with me. She shared with me that her deceased husband had come to her before she stepped into the labyrinth and walked with her. She hadn't told anyone else and thanked me for sharing the story and the music. The next morning, another participant sought me out to tell me that she had recently lost two of her brothers and they had both walked the labyrinth with her. She thanked me also.

Over the years I have continued to be humbled by the appreciation people have shown for my use of sound in healing. The most exciting thing about the sound work I do today is that I have been innovative and have blended with my sound work some of the other therapies I learned many years earlier.

Frequently, I get "downloads" of inspiration to create new methods and protocols. I teach workshops to help people tap into the healing power of their own voices, and I teach basic introductory sound therapy courses and various other offerings, where I combine practices—such as EFT with sound and essential oils, heart-centered breathing with guided meditation, sound and Ho'oponopono (the Hawaiian forgiveness principle) in a quest to open peoples' hearts to more joy and gratitude. All the things that I learned as I healed and overcame my grief have been blended into who I am and what I offer.

At one point I received a powerful download about how I could use my vocal harmonic frequencies (also known as overtone singing, which is what Tom Kenyon does) to activate DNA and clear fear that we have inherited. I combine this with essential oils and a special EFT tapping script to reprogram the cells and the DNA, and then I add in a short sound bath to take participants into a deeply relaxed state. The feedback from these sessions has been very positive, with people returning repeatedly, since they find that the effects are so beneficial.

My individual sessions attract many clients who have struggled with trauma and abuse. My personal experience recovering from these issues and my continual investigation into more ways to assist my clients to heal and grow also helps me heal and grow.

Clients also come to me to help resolve sleep problems, suppressed anger, depression, and dealing with major transitions such as starting a new career or ending a relationship. I have personal experience in all of these areas! I include Reiki with the sound work in every individual session and very often I include special essential oil blends to aid the clearing and healing process.

I firmly believe that sound (and all the other modalities from which I draw inspiration) do not heal anyone. They simply clear blockages and imbalances and reset the nervous system to its "rest and digest" mode so that an individual's self-healing process can take place.

Ultimately, our bodies are designed to heal from anything, but with a toxic environment including toxic water, air, food, and emotions, it is difficult for our bodies to do their job without some outside support. Sound is a wonderful support for our physical, emotional, mental, and spiritual bodies. It has been an important part of my healing journey and I am glad it's something I can offer to the world.

Epilogue

Why did Lucy seem to "endorse" Dan? My instincts had warned me that something wasn't right long before his abusive behavior showed itself.

Yet each time I asked her to let me know if she approved of him, Lucy encouraged me to continue down the road to marriage. Even her utter excitement at finding out that she would be a bridesmaid, at our wedding, although it really surprised me, further demonstrated her approval of the plan.

How could she, such a good judge of character, in my opinion, have been so deceived? Or was she? As my greatest teacher, Lucy helped to usher me into a pressure cooker of learning. I was confronted with all my insecurities and prejudices. I was metaphorically thrown into a furnace, which burned away all my pride and judgementalism.

Yet, from these ashes I emerged to experience unconditional love and to see Lucy in her full, magnificent self. Only then could I also see my magnificent self. This empowered me to draw a line in the sand and take the necessary steps to extricate myself from an abusive situation. I do not need to learn that lesson again.

Thank you, dearest Lucy, my greatest teacher and guru, for your patience with me. For 10 long years I struggled and doubted myself, losing and regaining my confidence. Thank you for your unconditional love which, in turn, allowed me to experience it fully for the very first time. I'm still learning to practice it in my daily life, and learning not to judge myself, or the people and situations with which I'm confronted. But it becomes easier with time and whenever I tune into you, I sense your loving presence around me, and my heart expands.

Addendum: A Special Needs Toolkit

Beliefs and other tools to help manage life as the parent of a special needs child

My belief that "everything happens for a reason" and that our reason for life is to learn and grow—to evolve—helped me move through the grieving process to acceptance much more smoothly than some other parents I knew. Also, the idea of reincarnation really resonates with me. I have experienced déjà vu strongly, several times in my life, in particular on my world travels. Some places like Luxor Temple in Egypt felt very familiar. I knew I had been there as a priest or priestess.

When I trekked the Inca Trail to Machu Picchu in Peru, at one point in the journey, a surge of energy passed through me and I burst into tears as I cried, "I'm home, I'm finally home." My heart swelled with love for that place. My affinity for Chile and Argentina and the ease with which I was able to learn and communicate in Spanish, makes me suspect I have lived there before.

Embracing this philosophy that we live more than once and, not only that, but we also choose who will be our parents, what country we will be born in, and roughly how our life will pan out, helped me to accept Lucy's confined existence.

I believe Lucy came specifically to teach me many things, the most important of which was how to give and receive unconditional love. She didn't need her father to stick around, she didn't need a long life. She has been the biggest teacher in my life, helping me learn things that have allowed me to help many others in my healing work.

The traumas I suffered, and the grief, were ways for me to grow and evolve. They were challenges to overcome. Some of this I already knew during Lucy's life and since then, I have developed a lot more clarity about the true extent of what I learned from her.

When I think about the unconditional love I felt for Lucy just before she died, I realize that although I felt great love for her throughout her life—strong enough to lead me to do extraordinary things and push myself beyond what I thought were my limits—it wasn't unconditional love in the sense of what I later experienced.

I realized that I had still perceived her through the lens of her limitations. I loved the vulnerable child, and this set me up to feel a heavy burden of responsibility for her well-being. What if I had considered her as a Creator Being, capable of manifesting what she needed?

The old saying that, "we are not physical beings having a spiritual experience but spiritual beings having a physical experience," became perfectly clear to me in those final weeks of Lucy's life.

I now see that unconditional love is present when we fully recognize this quality in another person. The gift lay in realizing that Lucy coming into my life was not about me "fixing" and changing her, but realizing that she had come to change me, for the better, in countless ways.

I wish this gift of insight on every parent of a child with special needs. However, I can see that cultural programming and beliefs can potentially keep us from reaching this point. I reside in a multicultural society where some traditions view disability as a curse that brings shame on the family.

Special needs children are often hidden from sight. There is not an emphasis on integrating them into mainstream schools the way it was done in Australia.

Young children, I believe, are naturally telepathic so I'm sure Lucy was communicating with her peers.

At the childcare center that she attended, one of the children, a young boy, insisted on taking his Elmo doll to the center because Lucy had told him she wanted to see it.

She became excited and animated when he presented it to her. Cultures where this mingling between differently abled children is not facilitated or encouraged, forces them to miss the richness of these interactions.

Growing up in Australia in the 1960s when there was no integration, I recall seeing school buses from the Spastic Children's Society passing by as the children with cerebral palsy in wheelchairs were transferred to an institution.

As a child, and even into adulthood, I was frightened or intimidated at the sight of these children if I ever came across them in public. It was such a joy to see the children at the childcare center and local school embrace Lucy as one of their own.

In hindsight, I can see that the fact that Lucy was so physically disabled meant that no one—not me nor the school system—put any expectations on her to conform to the "system."

Lucy could be likened to a "free agent," able to connect with the other children in a unique way.

Indulge me for a moment. If she really were an enlightened guru and she was capable of communicating great wisdom and insight telepathically, would she have wanted to experience life in a "normal" body and have to endure all the usual growing pains of other children, being bullied and picked on, influenced by peer pressure to conform, coerced into competing to achieve material success? She managed to avoid all of this and more!

I mentioned earlier that I believe that unconditional love is about accepting what is and not trying to change it.

I now look at this in the context of Eckhart Tolle's concept of living in the now.

His philosophy is not to waste time raging against what is, shouting that it should not be this way. He considers this to be insanity.

> *"Accept – then act. Whatever the present moment contains, accept it as if you had chosen it. Always work with it, not against. Make it your friend and ally, not your enemy. This will miraculously transform your whole life."[iii]*

This is a quote from the book, *The Power of Now*. I think Lucy may have had this understanding and this helped her to have no fear.

Basically, I am an optimistic person.

My depression, thankfully, didn't last too long and I managed to pick myself up and make the best of my circumstances. This helped me to have plenty of resilience, an essential skill when parenting a child with special needs.

Parenting a Child Like Lucy: What I Wish I'd Known:

Tip #1 – Highly Sensitive People, Empaths

In recent years I have learned about Highly Sensitive People and Empaths. Once I realized that I am an extremely sensitive Empath, it was a huge relief.

Rather than judging myself harshly, I now understood the mechanism leading to feelings of overwhelm and I have learned strategies for coping with a highly sensitive nervous system.

Armed with this knowledge back then, I might have managed some of the stress and overwhelm in better ways. I can recommend the books by Elaine Aron, *The Highly Sensitive Person,* and *The Highly Sensitive Child.* Many children with disabilities, particularly those with autism, are highly sensitive. Their behaviors can be misunderstood, if not viewed in this context. The books give plenty of practical advice and strategies to cope with a highly sensitive nervous system.

Lucy was also a highly sensitive Empath. Knowing what I know now, I would have recognized some of her crying as overwhelm and looked for ways to reduce her stimulation and so avoid pushing her into overwhelm.

Tip #2 – Energy Psychology Techniques (EFT and Emotion Code)

I wish I had known about energy psychology techniques such as EFT (Emotional Freedom Techniques) and Emotion Code back then. Emotion Code helps to clear any trapped emotions we may have in our body, and this helped me clear a lot of my stress and trauma, but this is not something to do on your own—a trained facilitator must conduct your sessions. I was fortunate to find a skilled practitioner who worked online and who helped me clear my own emotions and also those I had absorbed from others—even as far back as my childhood. EFT, on the other hand, is very easy to learn and has been a great "self-help" tool that I have used many times since I learned it. Stress can be nipped in the bud right when it is just starting to mount.

YouTube is a great resource for EFT instructions. Just search under "EFT" and whatever issue you are feeling, for example guilt, anger, shame, frustration, or grief, and you will find that someone will have posted a short segment, usually under 10 minutes, to guide you through a tapping sequence. One of my favorite EFT practitioners is Brad Yates, who has literally hundreds of videos posted on YouTube. I love his humor and his perceptiveness, and he comes across as wise and kind; his YouTube offerings have really helped me.

Here is a link to his channel:

https://www.youtube.com/user/eftwizard

Tip #3 – Shaking Medicine

I learned about Bradford Keeney and his wonderful book, *Shaking Medicine*, about six years ago. This man discovered the power of shaking as a mechanism for releasing stress quite accidentally when he was still a teenager. He decided to research it further and uncovered shaking traditions in several cultures worldwide such as the Kalahari Bushmen in Africa and the early Quakers. Wild animals naturally shake and shudder after experiencing stress to burn off the stress hormones and reset their nervous systems. We humans, and also animals kept in zoos, are the only mammals that do not do this spontaneously. When we don't shake off our fear in the moment, it solidifies into trauma.

Now that I have learned this simple technique, I use it if stress starts to build up in my body. Just a few minutes of letting go of control and shaking it all out has a profoundly relaxing effect on me. If I had known about shaking when I was filled with stress and tension during Lucy's lifetime, it may have helped me sleep more soundly and snap out of my depression more easily. If you have not tried it, give it a go. You do not need to buy the book to get started.

Here's a link to a video on Bradford Keeney and his work: https://www.youtube.com/watch?v=sGt1L7QXSDw

Tip #4 – Trauma and Tension Releasing Exercises

TRE® Tension and Trauma Releasing exercises were introduced to me by the Emotion Code practitioner who helped me so much. This is shaking in a particular way, releasing trauma held in the psoas muscle, deep inside the pelvis.

When you put the psoas muscle under stress by doing certain exercises, it begins to tremble and shake as it releases long-held trauma and stress.

For someone who needs a practitioner to guide them in shaking out stress and trauma, this is a wonderful technique. When I tried to release trauma using the technique, it was so intense that I became overwhelmed.

The therapist needed to modify the technique for me so I could do it more gently. I really appreciated having her to support me with this technique.

Here is a link to a video explaining it:

https://www.youtube.com/watch?v=67R974D8swM

And here is a link to the website where you can locate a trained practitioner in your area: https://www.tre.org/

Tip #5 – HeartMath Heart-Centered Breathing Technique

When my brother suffered a heart attack, his investigations into natural healing led him to the HeartMath Institute and I soon embraced their practices as well.

I was fascinated by how quickly and simply their heart-centered breathing technique could calm my mind and bring me into a state of peace. A lot of scientific research has been done on how this breathing technique—which focuses on imagining the breath is coming in and out of the heart center—can positively affect the health of the physical heart while reducing emotional stress.

Just a few minutes of breathing this way brings the brain and the heart into coherence, quieting the mental chatter and switching the nervous system back into the parasympathetic "rest and digest" mode. It also creates a strong electromagnetic field around the heart that can be measured. When several people in a room together practice the technique, their combined coherent fields can quickly affect a stressed person entering the room and bring them into coherence as well, without the need for them to do the heart-centered breathing technique themselves.

I am sure this could have helped me with my insomnia and also calmed the frantic thinking I often did about whether I was doing the right thing when I was worrying about Lucy. I regularly teach this technique to my stressed and traumatized clients, and I also use it myself while listening to them pour out their problems. It stops me from becoming overwhelmed by their distress and creates a coherent field of energy emanating from my heart-center that calms their nervous system simply because of their close proximity to my coherent electromagnetic field. If I had been able to create a strong coherent field around my heart when Lucy was upset, this would have helped to calm her down.

Here is a link to the website for the HeartMath Institute: https://www.heartmath.org/

Tip #6 – Sound Therapy: Crystal Singing Bowls

The first time I attended a "sound bath" with crystal singing bowls at a five-day wellness festival in Australia, I was profoundly affected. Although I was lying on the ground with just a tarpaulin between me and the hard earth, I was taken into the deepest, most relaxed state of my life. I was truly gob-smacked and intrigued. I returned each day of the festival for another sound bath and was equally transported every time. I fell in love with crystal singing bowls. They could completely switch off my busy mind and take me into a deep sleep. Alternatively, I could remain consciously aware, but in an altered state, where only my right brain was awake. Without the judgement, worry and analysis of the left brain, I was in bliss and total peace.

I urge anyone who has never tried a sound bath with crystal singing bowls to go and experience it. Recordings are second best, but very convenient when I am lying awake at night and sleep eludes me. I find that if I play my album, *"Celestial Garden,"* I fall fast asleep very quickly. I used several different sound tools on this album, along with my crystal bowls and my voice to create frequencies to entrain the brainwaves down into *theta* (dreaming sleep) and *delta* (deep sleep),

I find the sound of crystal singing bowls quite magical and more recently, I have discovered the crystal harp and crystal singing pyramids. There is something very special about quartz as a material for creating powerfully healing sounds. The sounds have a very long sustain, with certain crystal bowls and pyramids still vibrating for up to two minutes after I stop playing them. As sounds slowly fade, the brain latches onto the decaying sound, and it starts to quieten. This is one of the ways these instruments calm the nervous system. Another is the fact that they pulse at around one cycle per second, which is equivalent to very slow delta brainwaves in deep, deep sleep. If I had known about sound therapy during Lucy's life, it would certainly have helped me drop off to sleep. The parents of several of the special needs children I work with play my album every night at bedtime to help their child fall asleep.

Tip #7 – Sound Therapy: Biofield Tuning

The most recent sound therapy technique I have learned is Biofield Tuning. Eileen McKusick, a massage therapist, started experimenting one day with some tuning forks she had been given and what evolved was the most powerful sound therapy technique I have experienced so far. She found that the electromagnetic field that surrounds each of us contains energy distortions that correspond to traumas we have experienced. The theory is that when we are emotionally or physically traumatized through sporting injuries, car accidents, or other experiences, a part of us cannot cope and it dissociates. It ends up in the biofield, the electromagnetic field around us, which reaches about two meters on either side of us and one meter in front and behind us. By "combing" through the biofield with tuning forks, we can locate these distortions. The coherent frequency of the tuning fork dissolves the incoherent distortion that is holding the soul fragment in place. It can then be brought back into the body where it belongs.

What has surprised me and the many clients I work with, is that even if we have done the emotional work to heal our traumas, these fragments are still out in the field. It takes a lot of life force energy to maintain the distortions that hold the fragments, so once they are dissolved, we have much more energy for enjoying life. Most people find that they feel lighter after a session, and more peaceful.

I was very surprised to find that my birth trauma– in which both Mum and I almost died–had affected almost every part of my biofield. It has taken more work to clear that trauma from my biofield than both the trauma of being Lucy's mum and being married to my abusive ex-husband combined. I consistently find that the traumas we suffer as children take more effort to dissolve than adult traumas. Since learning the technique, I have not had an opportunity to use it on special needs children, but, intuitively, I feel that they would benefit greatly if their biofields were cleared of traumas, especially if they suffered from birth trauma and from issues in their early lives. This technique works very well when done remotely, so there is no need for the child to be physically present or lie down and stay still throughout the session.

To learn more, here is the link to the Biofield Tuning website: https://www.biofieldtuning.com/what-is-biofield-tuning

Tip #8 – Craniosacral Therapy

Due to the damage sustained in my neck from my forceps delivery, I have suffered with spinal issues from a young age. Chiropractic adjustments helped but sometimes, after just a few days, the bones would jam up again. When I discovered craniosacral therapy, a very gentle approach with no cracking of joints, I was amazed to find that the improvements to my spine lasted much longer and created far better outcomes than with chiropractic adjustments.

For a time, I was part of a team of therapists conducting rehabilitation camps for special needs children and for the duration of the camp, each child received a one-hour session of craniosacral therapy each day. I was amazed how even the most hyperactive children and those with every kind of disability, responded very positively to this form of therapy. It would have been wonderful to use this on Lucy and seen how it could have helped her.

To learn more, here is a link to the Biodynamic Craniosacral Therapy Association of North America website:

https://www.craniosacraltherapy.org/

Tip #9 – Mindfulness, Living in the Present Moment

My biggest regret after Lucy passed away was recognizing the amount of time I had spent worrying about the future– all a waste of time!

When I later came across the concepts of mindfulness, of being in the present moment, instead of incessantly thinking about the past or speculating about the future, I learned that the only time we can truly be at peace is when we are in the present moment, right here, right now. This is actually what happened near the end of Lucy's life, when I bathed her, and it became a sacred act.

I was so present that all the turmoil of my life simply faded away. The peace and awe I felt was magnificent.

It was only later, when I studied *A Course in Miracles* and *The Power of Now*, that I understood what had happened spontaneously during the bath times and learned ways to actively bring myself into the present moment.

Mindfulness practices are useful for any parent of a child with special needs to learn. They don't require us to put aside special time to do the practice. In Tolle's book, he explains that just paying attention to our breath, in and out, not trying to control it, just noticing it for 30 seconds, and doing this many times a day, is more beneficial than dedicating an hour to meditation.

I have practiced this while waiting for the elevator at my apartment, waiting for a red light to change while driving, brushing my teeth, and washing the dishes. The more we notice the breath, the calmer we become and the clearer our thoughts become.

Acknowledgements

Firstly, I wish to thank Judy Cockram who first suggested I write this book and even gave me the title! I didn't see her for a couple of years but when we met again, the first thing she asked was, "Have you written the book yet?" I hadn't even started it by then. Thanks for pestering me!

I wish to thank my dear friend, Karen Radzi for the use of her beautiful jungle home where I wrote most of the manuscript on my weekly writing retreats. The peaceful environment seemed to inspire me, and the words simply flowed onto the pages. I am also grateful to her for her insightful suggestions after reading the first draft. We discussed it for hours during which additional memories resurfaced and found themselves onto these pages.

A huge thanks to my friend, Virginia Kennedy, who read the first draft carefully, asking many questions and making lots of suggestions. This really helped to expand and develop the narrative.

I had attempted to write my story several times, hitting dead ends, before pleading with the Universe for a way to find some professional guidance. Soon after, I met Susan Crossman, a professional book coach and editor, who completely understood what I was trying to do and developed an outline, which became my roadmap to structure the narrative. This framework was invaluable to me, and her editing expertise added the final touches. This book would not have been possible without her. My thanks also to Michael Davie and Manor House for believing in me and publishing my story.

Finally, I want to thank my gorgeous daughter Lucy, my guru in disguise, who hovered around me throughout the writing process, always with her loving presence urging me to delve deep, to be honest with myself, and through this process, learn and grow even more. Thank you, thank you, thank you from the bottom of my heart.

Books Mentioned in the Narrative:

A Course in Miracles by Helen Shucman

Annie's Coming Out by Rosemary Crossley

Awakened by Autism: Embracing Autism, Self and Hope for a New World by Andrea Libutti MD

The Aware Baby by Aletha Solter

Eight Feet in the Andes: Travel with a Mule from Ecuador by Dervla Murphy

Empath's Survival Guide: Life Strategies for Sensitive People by Judith Orloff

The Highly Sensitive Child by Elaine Aron

The Highly Sensitive Person by Elaine Aron

Illusions by Richard Bach

Jonathan Livingston Seagull by Richard Bach

Out on a Limb by Shirley MacLaine

The Power of Now by Eckhart Tolle

Seth Speaks, by Jane Roberts

Shaking Medicine: The Healing Power of Ecstatic Movement by Bradford Keeney

The Lost Cities series by David Hatcher Childress

The Temple of Man by R.A. Schwaller de Lubicz

Notes

[i] Wikipedia: https://en.wikipedia.org/wiki/Rosemary_Crossley

[ii] https://en.wikipedia.org/wiki/TaKeTiNa_Rhythm_Process

[iii] Eckhart Tolle, *The Power of Now*, (Hachette Livre Australia Pty Limited, Sydney, 2004), pp 35-36

Working with Elizabeth Huxtable

Elizabeth Huxtable offers individual sessions, either online or in person and can be contacted via her website: https://scientificsoundasia.com/

Email: elizabeth@scientificsoundasia.com

Workshops and training sessions are listed on:

- Facebook: Scientific Sound Asia

  https://www.facebook.com/scientificsoundasia

- Instagram: ScientificSound.Asia

  https://www.instagram.com/scientificsound.asia/

Albums are downloadable via Bandcamp:

https://elizabethhuxtable.bandcamp.com/

Manor House
905-648-4797
www.manor-house-publishing.com